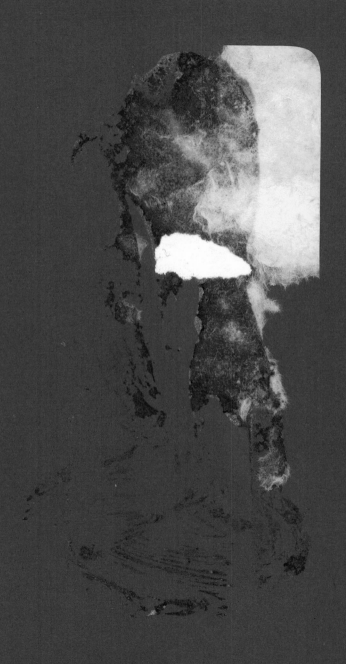

THE VOICES

By Joseph Wechsberg:

LOOKING FOR A BLUEBIRD

HOMECOMING

BLUE TROUT AND BLACK TRUFFLES

THE SELF-BETRAYED

THE BEST THINGS IN LIFE

JOURNEY THROUGH THE LAND OF ELOQUENT SILENCE

THE MERCHANT BANKERS

VIENNA, MY VIENNA

Joseph Wechsberg

THE VOICES

1969
DOUBLEDAY & COMPANY, INC., GARDEN CITY, NEW YORK

My gratitude to William Shawn who published a substantial portion of this book in *The New Yorker*.

Library of Congress Catalog Card Number 69–18102

To my brave friends in Prague—and to
our memories of the unforgettable "Prague Spring"

On my last trip to Czechoslovakia, before it all happened, I arrived in Prague on August 5, 1968, the day after the Bratislava Declaration. It seems like ages now. Nearly everybody I talked to was *zklámán* (disappointed). A feeling of hangover was in the air, after the exhilaration of the preceding week, during the summit meeting at Čierná nad Tisou, when the entire population had rallied behind the leaders of Czechoslovakia. (The August 21 issue of *Roháč*, a satirical Slovak weekly, that was on the stands when the invasion came, shows a man behind a typewriter while another hands him a pair of rubber gloves. "Don't you know that since Bratislava you can't write about this country without your gloves?") The Declaration was signed at the Bratislava Hall of Mirrors where Talleyrand, on December 26, 1805, after Napoleon's victory at

Austerlitz, had signed the First Bratislava Peace Treaty with Emperor Franz of Austria. An old Czech friend (whom I shall call by the initial J.) reminded me gloomily that it had been a short-lived peace. He was an amateur historian, as so many others were in this beautiful, old city, with its violent history. He said that a step backward was to be expected after "the great experiment" of the "Prague Spring" which had started in January. "God knows how it's going to end but it was worth living through it." Speaking in the past sense he betrayed his pessimism and (as he later admitted) the fear that was always in the back of his mind. On an earlier visit, in July, I'd read an editorial in *Literární Listy*, the Writers' Union weekly, in which A. J. Liehm, a prominent Communist journalist, asked, "What's going to happen? Where is the worst danger? Does anyone really know how Czechoslovakia will look in two years, even approximately?"

The beerhouse statesmen at "U Fleků," the famous old tavern, claim that it all began at the Grenoble Winter Olympics when the Czechoslovak ice-hockey team beat the Russians, five to four. Actually, it all began on January 6, when the "reformers" under Alexander Dubček had ousted the "conservative" regime under Old-Stalinist Antonín Novotný. The reformers—writers, students, scientists, economists, and other intellectuals—were faithful Communists, but they wanted to make Communism more human, combining Eastern-style Socialism with Western-style democracy—a never before attempted blend. It had been in the air for a long time but when it came, at last, it seemed almost too good to be true. Liehm called it "the beautiful dream of freedom from which we never want to wake up."

I was in Czechoslovakia several times during that unforgettable spring. I'd been born in this country and lived there for the first thirty-two years of my life, before I came to America. In spite of war, persecution and several political purges, some of my old friends were still there, and we spent much time together during the intoxicating "Prague Spring" reminiscing and talking about the future. Suddenly Czechoslovakia, after its long and painful past, was finding again its national identity. The Czechs and Slovaks had been ridiculed for centuries under the Habsburg rule. After a brief spell of independence, they had been humiliated by the Nazis. They had become the Schweiks of this world, known to be cunning and realistic rather than heroic and romantic. Yet now, in the early months of the "Prague Spring," they were getting foolhardy. The memory of the Hussites—the greatest era in Czech history—became very much alive. Dubček was often compared to Jan Hus: neither man wanted to leave his Church, but only to reform it. Suddenly, there was freedom of the press, freedom to travel, freedom from fear. ("Only a nation that hasn't known freedom for twenty years loves freedom so dearly," wrote Zurich's *Weltwoche*.)

A sense of emancipation and a feeling of euphoria were spreading through the country. There was danger in all this, of course, but people didn't want to think of it. On May 13, *Práce*, the Trade Unions' paper, had asked Moscow "to deny rumors of an intervention." In the Soviet Union, the intellectuals began to listen to the voice of Prague. Novosibirsk's *Sowjetskaja Rossija* wrote that "dozens of scientists" had signed protests against the hard Kremlin line. The May issue of *Novy Mir* was published, in a reduced circulation, only in August. There were many arrests in the Ukrainian Soviet Republic which has sixty miles of a common border with Slovakia, and where Ruthenian broadcasts from Slovakia could be heard.

Last June 27, one day after the National Assembly (Parliament) had abolished censorship, *Literární Listy*, followed by other papers, published "Two Thousand Words," an appeal addressed to "workers, farmers, artists, scientists, technicians, and everyone . . . The inspiration came from the scientists." (Among the signers was Ludvík Vaculík, "who also wrote this text.") "Two Thousand Words," a great document of political freedom, was directed against the discredited conservatives,

3

"selfish and domineering people, reproachful cowards and people with bad conscience."

> Parliament forgot how to discuss, the government to govern, the directors to direct. Decisions had no meaning, laws lost their value, personal and collective honor collapsed. . . . The greatest deception of the rulers was that they presented their license as the will of the working class. Of course, no responsible person would believe the workers were guilty of such things. But the majority of the functionaries . . . still has the means of power in its hands, especially in outlying districts.

The appeal did "not overevaluate the significance of criticism from the ranks of writers and students," called economics "the source of social changes," and said there was "no reason for a sense of national victory, only the basis of new hope." It warned against the conservatives "who take advantage of the summer vacations when people desire to get away from it all . . . though we may bet that our dear opponents will not permit themselves a summer vacation . . . They will mobilize their obligated people and will try to arrange for a peaceful Christmas holiday." Clearly, the fear was in the back of everybody's mind. Then followed the paragraph that shocked all orthodox Communists,

> As nothing more can be expected from the present central political organs, more should be achieved on the district and community levels. Let us request the departure of people who misused their power, damaged public property, behaved dishonestly or cruelly. *We have to find out means of forcing them to resign,* e.g. by public criticism, resolutions, demonstrations, demonstrative work brigades, collections for contributions for their retirement, *strikes and boycott of their doors.* [The italics are mine.] On the other hand, we must refuse all unlawful methods as indecent and

4

rude, as these would be used for influencing Alexander Dubček. Our aversion to writing rude letters must be so general that as of now each letter of this kind they might receive could be considered a letter they had sent to themselves . . . *Let us establish committees for the protection of freedom of speech. Let us organize our own monitor service for such meetings.* If you happen to hear peculiar news, check it, send delegations to the competent authorities and make their answers publicly known. Support the security organs when they prosecute really criminal activities. It is *not our aim to induce anarchy* and a state of general insecurity. Avoid neighborhood squabbles. Do not get intoxicated with political matters. Expose snoopers.

For the first time, some of the reformers seemed unnerved. National Assembly president Josef Smrkovský called the appeal "a mistake." Dubček said that the Party did not go along with the proclamation. It was rumored that Dubček had lost his majority in the Presidium, and that the conservatives were getting ready to take over the mass media. Actually telex messages were sent to all Communist Party organizations: the Presidium was said to consider the proclamation "an attack against the Party." They were signed by Alois Indra, no Presidium member, a former railroad worker from Košice, Slovakia, the darling of the Soviets. Indra's speeches had been often played up by the Moscow press while Dubček's were played down.

Radio, television and all newspapers except *Rudé Pravo*, the Party organ, supported "Two Thousand Words" and called the official criticism "a tragic misunderstanding." Prime Minister Oldřich Černik saved the situation, in a resolute speech before Parliament, saying that the proclamation was certainly not an expression of counterrevolution, but the opinion of one segment of the Party. (The first mention of "counterrevolutionary elements," an ominous term, appeared in the July 11 issue of Moscow's *Pravda.*) Now even *Rudé Pravo* supported "Two Thousand Words," but the drama had started. Walter Ulbricht and Wladyslaw Gomulka accused the Prague reformers of "endangering the future of Socialism." ("Exactly a hundred and twenty years after the Communist Manifesto, the leaders of a well-armed 300-million nation seem to tremble because of a 2000-word editorial written by a non-member of the world literature establishment," wrote *Münchner Merkur* in Munich.) The stage was set for the Warsaw meeting in mid-July, to which the Czechoslovak leaders were not invited.

Many people in Prague wondered whether the "Warsaw Letter" would have been drafted to the "Dear Comrades" if the Soviets had known more about the true situation inside Czechoslovakia. "A little more understanding and trust, a better evaluation of the real situation, of how the people feel would have helped," *Literární Listy* wrote. "But the Soviet Embassy in Prague mistook extreme incidents as 'typical' and denounced the honesty of our leaders as mere 'tactics.'" Disenchanted young Communists in Prague began to speak of the Kremlin's "nineteenth-century colonial Communism." "How can Comrades Brezhnev, Suslov and Shelest understand our country which had an organized workers' movement ninety years ago, when their grandfathers probably were serfs under the Czars?" a Communist poet asked me.

The slogan "Neither Canossa nor Constance" was first heard in Prague. (In Constance, Jan Hus who had been promised by Emperor Sigismund an imperial safeguard guarantee, was arrested and burned at the stake.) The fine Slovakian hand of Alexander Dubček seemed to be behind the sudden decision to convoke a special plenary meeting of the Central Committee that would approve the Presidium's reply to the Warsaw Letter. The Soviets must not be able to claim that the reformers had drafted their reply "against the will of the Party." But Dubček was not sure of a two-thirds majority: there were still about forty Conservatives among the Central Committee's hundred and ten members. He was gambling on his strong popular support inside Czechoslovakia, and on the solidarity expressed by Marshal Tito, Nicolae Ceausescu, the Communist parties of Italy and France, and of most other countries in Western Europe. Opposing him were the West German Communists who had to follow the Ulbricht line, and the Communist parties of tiny Luxembourg and the United States of America. In East Berlin, a delegation of American comrades suggested watchfulness "with regard to support extended by the imperialist forces of the United States to the counterrevolutionary forces in Czechoslovakia," according to Ulbricht's Party paper, *Neues Deutschland.*

All regional Party organizations were alerted to have their already elected delegates for the next Party Congress (to be held on September 9) to stand by. If the Central Committee hadn't voted for Dubček, the reformers might have called the Congress the following day to elect a more liberal Central Committee. For the first time, the press was permitted inside the Central Committee building. Eighty-eight members accepted the reply unconditionally; twenty-one excused themselves. The Warsaw Letter had been written in unmistakable Party jargon. The reply from Prague was drafted in a clear, lucid style; the reformers had reformed even the political language.

Many observers in Prague wondered whether the Prague Party Presidium functioned as a collective coalition, somewhat as the Moscow Politburo. Most probably, the Prague group consisted of individuals, each of whom had certain functions. Dubček, the idea man and catalyst, seemed to develop the strategy and set the style. Instinctively or intentionally, he played down the position of the all-powerful First Party Secretary. Around him, several men formed the inner circle of power. Prime Minister Černik from Ostrava, Moravia, became Dubček's chief executive officer. Many people considered him the most brilliant among the reformers, and some called him the best Prime Minister since the great Antonín Švehla, who served in the early years of Masaryk's republic. Dubček was

7

credited with mysteriously finding the best available people. They set the new line, the mass media promoted it enthusiastically, and when the whole country followed, "the beautiful dream" seemed to come true. ("History is made, after all, by human beings, though the Soviets won't admit it," my friend J. said.)

Dubček also showed his genius by suggesting Army General Ludvík Svoboda for the office of President that had fallen low under Novotný who kept aloof from the people and traversed Prague in his black limousine, hiding behind Russian-style curtains and security. Svoboda was seen walking all by himself in the streets of Prague, and the people said it was almost *"jako za Masaryka,"* as under Masaryk. Svoboda, too, played his role in the inner circle. (In Moscow, during the hour of truth, he became no Pétain.) Then there was Smrkovský, a sort of *tribunus plebis,* Dubček's liaison man with the people, who loved to address large crowds and appeared unexpectedly to inspire confidence. Other inner-circle men were Party ideologist Čestmír Cisář and Interior Minister Josef Pavel, the first Communist Interior Minister anywhere whom his citizens liked and trusted. In all Eastern countries the Interior Ministry is the center of fear. Pavel forbade all wire-tapping, except after special permission by the General Procurator, and he appeared for questioning before a newly formed Military and Security Committee of the National Assembly. No Communist country ever before permitted such a committee to investigate the Interior Ministry, the center of secret-police actions. Nothing showed more dramatically the scope of Czechoslovakia's democratization.

The reformed Communist Party statute (on which the Party Congress was expected to vote) contained other dramatic innovations. It was said that henceforth a minority might stand on its interpretation provided it was not "contrary to the basic Party program." (Lenin's doctrine of Socialist centralism states unequivocally that once a question is settled by the majority, all dissenters must fall in line.) The principle of secret balloting for all Party bodies and functions was introduced. Joining or leaving the Party was to be a matter of everybody's free will. Each member would have the right to speak "openly and critically" about activities of the Party, its leaders, the Presidium and Central Committee, and all members, "irrespective of their function." No person was to hold more than one important office. (Novotný had been President and First Party Secretary.) Obviously, the Party's entire structure was to be changed. A leading political writer called it "truly a new Socialism, quite different from the Kremlin's petit-bourgeois Communism."

Late in July, the people of Czechoslovakia watched, with a terrifying sense of *déjà-vu*, the buildup of a colossal psychological warfare campaign. Well-publicized Soviet troop movements started from the western Ukraine and Poland, and from Saxony; large troop concentrations were massed along the borders of Slovakia, on the territory of Hungary; long columns of Red Army tanks and armored vehicles traveled across East Germany's *Autobahnen* at night, with dimmed lights; allied observers said there were a hundred thousand men in this area alone. From Brest, Terespol and Leipzig, heavy artillery and amphibian vehicles were going south. *Izvestia* wrote that "a sea of oil" was brought into the "maneuver area" by tank cars and helicopters. At this point, East Germany's A.D.N. press agency, always glad to oblige a friend, reported that Soviet Army General Sergej M. Shtemenko, one of Stalin's trusted advisers and East Germany's former military overlord, had replaced Army General Mikhail Kazakov as chief of staff of the Warsaw Pact forces. The Soviet press assured the "dear comrades" in Prague that the aim of the maneuvers was "the annihilation of all Western aggressors." To make matters worse, the West German military establishment, showing bad timing and bad judgment, announced its *own* maneuvers for September along Czechoslovakia's western borders where, thirty years ago, Hitler had massed the *Wehrmacht* before meeting with Neville Chamber-

9

lain in Munich. The maneuvers were called off only after the propagandists of *Pravda* had made the most of "West German revanchism."

By the end of July, at least twenty-eight Soviet divisions, supported by other Warsaw Pact forces, had completely surrounded the "fraternal" Socialist Republic of Czechoslovakia. Meanwhile, the Czechoslovak Army (175,000 men) were restricted to their barracks or kept near drill grounds. The Prague Ministry of Defense contributed a bit of cheerful news by estimating that it would take the brotherly Soviet forces "two hours and forty-six minutes" to occupy the country's nerve centers. (They were not very wrong.) Even after August 10, when the maneuvers had ended, most of the troops remained not far from the borders of Czechoslovakia. I asked a Czech colonel, a former classmate of mine, whether they would fight the Red Army. He threw up his hands as if to indicate that he found my question impossible to answer. "The Poles have fought against the Russians for centuries, and the East Germans and many Hungarians fought against them during the Second World War," he said. "But many of our senior officers fought on the side of the Red Army, and we have close friends among the Soviet officers . . . It would be a terrible emotional dilemma." It turned out to be worse than that.

The strategy of terror became evident in other ways, too. Soviet tourists were not permitted to travel to Prague but all over the country Russian visitors, mostly strong young men, were arriving who looked nothing like tourists. They came in gray buses or in Volga cars equipped with two-way radios. An "American" arms cache was "discovered" in Sokolov, near the Bavarian (West German) and Saxonian (East German) borders. "All they neglected to include was a card, 'From the CIA, with compliments to A. Dubček for twenty years of faithful service,'" a Czech told me. The Czech police announced that the weapons were covered with East German oil, as a protection against rust. Once again, the German *Gründlichkeit* (thoroughness) proved embarrassing. An East Berlin radio station announced, in Czech, that Prague stores were being plundered and Dubček had lost control of the country. The situation in Czechoslovakia was described as "threatening." ("Threatening whom?", some of my friends asked sarcastically.) *Literární Listy* reprinted a sentence from the protocol of Poland's Central Committee, in October 1956, "I'm told that large Soviet troop movements were reported along our borders and inside the country, that tank columns were seen near Bratislava." The people of Czechoslovakia reacted with astonishing calm. There was no hoarding of foodstuffs; the banks reported no unusual withdrawals of money. Americans were assured by their Czech acquaintances that they quite understood American non-interference. Some even argued that the American-Soviet détente might keep the Soviets from any rash action. ("During the 'Prague Spring,' we were like people in love, ready to believe *anything*," my friend J. said later.) In the countryside, the Soviet maneuver troops requisitioned food from the populace; they gave receipts in Czech and Russian and promised payment "later." A cartoon in *Literární Listy* showed a Soviet general telling his fellow generals, "Hard to tell, comrades, I saw democratic Socialism only from a tank." During the meeting in Čierná nad Tisou, another cartoon showed the Czech Lion (the national symbol) walking on a tightrope. Soviet Academician F. Konstantinov attacked Cisář who had doubted the supremacy of Leninism over Marxism—heresy! Marshal Tito was rumored to keep his jet ready on the island of Brioni to be in Prague "at three hours' notice." The Prague Radio reported that the dismissed friends of ex-President Novotný were "in their homes, summer houses and at the Russian Black Sea . . . waiting." Everybody seemed to be living in Kafka's unreal no man's land. No one saw the handwriting on the wall when a Sofia newspaper, *Vecherne Noviny,* asked whether Reinhard Heydrich's "shadow of blood" would again appear over Czechoslovakia.

Lord Bertrand Russell, in a message to Kosygin, expressed his sympathy for the Prague reformers.

On the afternoon of July 25, Pavel Kohout, a well-known Communist writer, was talking with three friends at the editorial offices of *Literární Listy*. A slight sense of defeatism seemed to be spreading through the country, prior to the meeting of the Czechoslovak and Soviet leaders. Kohout later wrote that he'd felt rather *úzko* (anxious). Somebody suggested to print, and sign, an appeal to their country's leaders to remain firm. They wanted Vaculík to write it but the author of "Two Thousand Words" didn't want to become typed as an appeal specialist. ("I suppose Vaculík was reluctant to start the Third World War," Kohout said.) So he himself wrote the "Appeal to the Party Presidium" which appeared that evening in a special edition of *Literární Listy*. The front page showed a well-known photograph, "Burial of a Red Army Soldier, 1945," a poem by Jaroslav Seifert, and Kohout's moving plea,

> Once again, our homeland has become the cradle of hope, not for us alone. . . . We can bring evidence that Socialism is not just an emergency solution for the developing countries but the only genuine alternative for the whole of civilization. We hoped that this fact would be welcomed by the Socialist camp. Instead, we are being accused of treason, of crimes which we didn't commit. . . . Comrades, it is your historic duty to forestall this danger. All that we are striving for can be summed up in four words: Socialism! Alliance! Sovereignty! Freedom!"

In Czech, these last four words all begin with "S" (*Socialismus! Spojenectví! Suverenita! Svoboda!*) which created a powerful alliteration.

Not all of you have the same opinion on everything. Some of you are sharply criticized for pre-January

12

mistakes. . . . But nobody wishes to change this criticism into a vendetta. It would be tragic if the private feelings of any one of you were to prevail over the responsibility which you at this moment bear for 14,-361,000 people . . . Be united! We believe in you!

All over the country, people queued up to sign the Appeal, putting down their names *and* addresses, in the full knowledge that they might be signing up for a free trip to the nearest jail. ("I was pleased," said Kohout. "This would later save the police much work." How right he was!) Signing the Appeal became a demonstration of national unity, "the spontaneous expression of people with different beliefs, acting from different viewpoints, supporting the leadership for the same purpose," as Premier Černik later said. "We were lining up for freedom," my friend J. remembers wistfully.

On Sunday morning, July 28, an acquaintance of mine drove through a small, deserted village in Southern Bohemia. Most of the men were at home, the women were at Mass. As he reached the village square, he saw an old peasant and his two sons carry their best table out of the house, set it up on the sidewalk, and lay a stack of white paper on it. Suddenly, the village square was filled with men. They came from everywhere, formed a line, and began signing their names to the "Appeal." The old peasant asked them to write legibly so there would be no *švindl*—that is to say, no charges of misrepresentation. Mass was over, the women signed up, too. They reported that the Catholic priest had asked the congregation to pray with him for Comrade Dubček. The village must have had its feuds and jealousies, but that morning they were all united. It was the same story all over the country: Czechs and Moravians and Slovaks signed, and members of the minorities. Almost two million signatures were collected. Every seventh person in the country signed the Appeal. In Prague, East German tourists asked to be permitted to sign; some were interviewed by Prague television reporters standing right next to their cars with the East German license plates visible, as though they never wanted to go home again. In Můstek, close to Wenceslas Square, a large sign said, "'VIVA DUBČEK AND HIS BOYS!" A Fund of the Republic was established, enterprises donated surplus profits, and individual citizens made a symbolic donation of one gram of gold. I know a dear old lady who had never liked "those Communists," but now she queued up too, "to give some gold for Dubček." In its first week, the Fund accumulated three million dollars.

On July 27th, two days before Dubček left for his meeting with the Soviet leaders at Čierná, he made a short eloquent appeal to his people. He was convinced that "our friends will realize, though not necessarily at once, that our renascent Socialist process is no threat to their interests," and thanked the people for their "confidence." He promised not to retreat a single step and said the objective of the present government was "to endow Socialism with the human face which rightly belongs to it." As Dubček left the television studio, two students handed him a sheet of papers with signatures, and Dubček laughed. An American who has lived in Prague for a long time told me, "There was a look in people's eyes that I've never seen before. These sober, realistic Czechs had suddenly become romantic idealists. They knew the risks and didn't give a damn. It was crazy. It was wonderful!"

On Sunday night, Kohout took a large briefcase home that contained the signatures of 85,509 people. He felt like celebrating, but then he thought of the *Closely Watched Trains* (a famous Czech film) in Čierná, and he didn't celebrate. He took the papers into his bedroom ("tonight there was no room on earth with so many people in it") and the next morning he took them to *Literární Listy*. "They should be put into a chest and placed in Dubček's office, and if once again someone comes and says something, Dubček should just get up and open that chest."

As the talks dragged on in the watched trains and there was

14

no news, "Čierná" took on the ominous meaning of "Munich" and some people began to think of "Budapest." Even now, few people except those who attended the Čierná meeting know what happened there, and they won't talk. It was rumored in Prague that P. Y. Shelest, the Ukrainian Party boss and a strong Politburo hawk, viciously attacked Dubček; that either Kosygin or Brezhnev viciously attacked František Kriegel, a doctor and head of the National front, whom they contemptuously called "that Galician Jew." (Obviously, Čierná was not Glassboro.) Twice it was said, the meeting was saved by President Ludvik Svoboda, who refused to accede to a Soviet demand for stationing Soviet soldiers in Czechoslovakia, insisted on his country's sovereignty, and told the Politburo that the Czechoslovak Communist Party was in firm control of the country. Brezhnev began to weep and embraced Svoboda, who is that *rara avis* in modern history—a general who is also a statesman. At one point Brezhnev got so furious at Dubček, his old classmate from the Party Cadre College in Moscow, that he had to lie down. Some people in Prague said, perhaps hopefully, that Brezhnev had suffered a slight heart attack.

In Prague, meanwhile, the suspense became almost unbearable. My friend J. thinks that Dubček and his boys lost their sense for time and space in Čierná where they were completely cut off from their own people. Later, the laconic communiqué was an anticlimax, and people became even more skeptical when the Bratislava summit meeting was announced for August 3rd. Some optimists thought that the meeting was an elaborate face-saving device, to help the Soviet Politburo vis-à-vis its Warsaw Pact partners. The optimists were encouraged when they saw the Communist leaders that night on their television screens at a wreath-laying ceremony, where they looked solemn but brotherly, and now there was no doubt that soft-hearted Comrade Brezhnev was crying: we all saw it on television. (And four weeks later the soft-hearted Comrade told Svoboda in Moscow that he would "smother the counter-

15

revolution in a sea of blood"—with no tears in his eyes, it is said in Prague.)

The next morning, the optimists woke up and were no longer that, after trying to decode the Bratislava Declaration, a document of scientific ambiguity, written in the Byzantine clichés of the Kremlin. Nearly every statement was neutralized by an anti-statement. The fraternal parties "resolutely stressed the need for undivided solidarity and exceptional vigilance," but they would also do everything possible "toward preservation of national sovereignty and independence." (And approximately at the same time Marshal Gretchko and his generals were cleaning up the last details for the invasion of Czechoslovakia and the end of its national sovereignty.) Dubček and his boys might find hope, whatever it was worth, in the sentence, "Each fraternal party solves its problems . . . taking into consideration specific national conditions." In the tortuous history of the double cross, the Bratislava Declaration will rank close to the Molotov-Ribbentrop Pact. But then, it is doubtful whether Dubček learned the true story of the Molotov-Ribbentrop Pact at the Party Cadre College in Moscow.

The people in Prague, no fools, began to worry about the things the Bratislava Declaration did *not* say rather than those it said. Prime Minister Černik admitted in a Party meeting that it was "not as accentuated as we see things here." Smrkovský admitted, less diplomatically, that one had agreed to stop "mutual polemics" (of which not a word was said in the Declaration). The East Berlin papers helpfully explained that the Czechoslovak delegation had agreed "to secure the political direction [read: censorship] of press, radio and television, in the spirit of Socialism." The reticent Declaration said nothing about that, even in its smallest print. Ideologist Cisář asked the journalists "to consider the interests of State and Party" and to show "a statesmanlike sense of response." Undaunted, the journalists replied they were not supposed to be statesmen; their sense of responsibility was ruled "not only by the Party." Oldřich Švestka, the conservative editor of *Rudé Pravo*, who had been accused by many of being all things to all men, wrote that "there were only victors in Bratislava, where each side won." (My friend J., the historian, reminded me of the Metternich conferences where neither side won.) Then Švestka, perhaps seeing the wave of the future at the far horizon, fired two progressive editors on the staff of his Party paper, perhaps to punish them for starting a palace revolution against him in the mad days of the "Prague Spring," when a *Rudé Pravo* editor wrote in *Literární Listy* about what went on in his paper. Looking back now, it all makes sense to me, but when I was there in Prague it didn't seem logical to anyone.

"It says in the Declaration we're going to keep our sovereignty," a man said. "Didn't we have sovereignty until now? We must remain, closer than before, in the Warsaw Pact. How can we attain a higher standard of living without help from the West which we must not accept? Prices and wages are rising, and everybody knows there is creeping inflation." My friend J. said, "We can only hope that the Soviet leadership will try to make a cautious step into the twentieth century. The other day I spoke to a Latvian who said he spent the holiday in 'the Soviet Union.' Imagine a Californian saying that he goes 'to the United States' for a holiday in New York." Many Czech Communists were offended by the Russians' inability to grasp their situation. "They ought to know by now that there is no private sector in our agriculture, industry, commerce as in East Germany and Poland; that until recently no non-Communist Western paper was for sale here as in Hungary and Romania. Belgrade's *Borba* was right when it spoke of the 'tragedy' in the minds of some Socialist leaders."

Tito had become a popular hero in Prague: back in 1948, he had been read out of the Soviet bloc, and he got away with it. (Also, his country is *not* located between the Soviet Union and West Germany as is Czechoslovakia.) When the people in Prague shouted "Dub-*ček!* Ti-*to!*" they wanted Dubček to become a Tito and not, God forbid, a Gomulka. A few days later, they shouted, "Dub-*ček!* Ti-*to!* Ceau-ses-*cu!*" and in between they kept an eloquent, icy silence when the despised Ulbricht made a short appearance in Karlovy Vary, after Prague Radio told the people that silence can be more devastating than booing. When I left Prague, a few days later, everybody seemed to be sitting back and relaxing, for the first time in weeks. It was high time for a summer vacation. My friend J. said he was going to Paris with his wife, on a visit which they had twice postponed for political reasons. He thought nothing "serious" would happen now. Comrades Brezhnev and Podgorny had gone to the Black Sea. Llewellyn Thompson, the American Ambassador in Moscow, had gone to Italy. Willy Brandt was fishing in Norway. And on August 19, General Lyman Lemnitzer, the NATO military commander, had gone to Greece. "If anyone knows something, *he* must know it," my friend J. said, and bought his ticket for Paris. I went back to Vienna.

At 6 A.M. on Wednesday, August 21, I turned on the radio on my bedside table, as I often do, when I am waking up. I was still half asleep. There was the weather forecast, and then the announcer said, in his unperturbed voice and soft Viennese dialect, "At eleven o'clock last night, troops of the five Warsaw Pact states invaded Czechoslovakia . . . brutally violating all fundamental international and human rights. . . ." I was no longer asleep. At seven o'clock, I heard that tanks were said to be approaching the center of Prague. Radio Austria said it had tried, and failed, to call its correspondents in Prague. (At 4:05 A.M. the electric current had been turned off in the Interhotels of Prague where most correspondents live, and there was no telex service.) Radio Belgrade reported of "vast armies" moving into Czechoslovakia "from all directions." Radio Moscow broadcast its regular program, Viennese waltzes and the morning gymnastics. TASS reported the "fraternal aid measures" only at 7:45, and *Pravda* came out at noon instead of in the morning. I couldn't get Radio Prague

18

until it was almost eight o'clock. Then I heard a woman announcer saying that the troops were getting near the radio station. Her voice was well controlled, yet there was an undertone of deep emotion; women are often braver in such moments than men.

"They are going to silence our voices but they cannot silence our hearts," she said, with great emphasis. She added that everyone was *"za Dubčekem"* ("behind Dubček.") Another woman's voice said, "For God's sake, people, *klid a odvaha* (calm and courage)!" A man shouted, "They've surrounded the building. They're already in the courtyard! Listen!" He must have put the microphone to the open window. The staccato of machine-gun fire seemed very close. The news broadcast became an ear-witness report. I was probably as shocked as everybody else who listened in. Only a few days earlier, I'd agreed with an American diplomat in Prague that an intervention was definitely possible. (The American had been ridiculed as an alarmist by many of his diplomatic colleagues in Prague.) But it is one thing to discuss the possibility of an invasion and quite another to hear the shooting over the radio. Somehow, I'd always hoped against hope that it wouldn't *really* happen—the Russians shooting at some of their most loyal Allies! Only a year ago, you couldn't travel in this country without seeing banners proclaiming "Eternal Friendship with the Union of Soviet Socialist Republics" or "Side by Side with the Glorious Red Army."

The glorious Red Army was shooting with heavy guns, to judge by what I could hear, and there were also sounds of great confusion, but the woman announcer said, slowly, emphasizing every syllable, "They have entered the building, but we are still here, and we'll be with you, as long as we can hold out. . . . We are behind Dubček and we'll never give up, *never.*" Another woman was sobbing. Suddenly there was silence, and then I heard the Czech national anthem, *"Kde Domov Můj?"* "[Where is My Home?]" It is a sad and beautiful anthem, the only one I know that starts out with a question,

19

and I thought I'd never heard a truer answer to the question than a moment ago. The windows of our living room in Vienna where I was sitting face east. The air was very clear, with a trace of autumn, and I could see the faint line of the faraway hills beyond the Danube. Behind them was the land that had once been my home, too. I thought of the people there who were now listening to the anthem, like me, and weeping.

The Czech anthem was followed by the rousing, fighting Slovak anthem, "*Nad Tatrou se Blýská* [Over the Tatra Mountains There's Lightning]." Then there was silence. The phone rang. An Austrian friend called. He'd listened too and he was deeply moved. "Just like March 11, 1938, when [Chancellor] Schuschnigg came on the radio to say that Hitler's troops were about to invade Austria," he told me. "Schuschnigg said, 'God save Austria!' and they played the anthem, and that was the end." He hung up. It occurred to me that no one in Prague had said, "God save Czechoslovakia!" The realistic Czechs knew that God would save them only if they helped themselves.

At ten minutes past 10 A.M., on August 21, when Radio Prague stopped broadcasting, the occupation was already a military success and a political failure. People didn't know it yet; the details became known only several weeks later.

The TASS statement claiming that certain Czechoslovak leaders had "called" for the Warsaw Pact forces, has never been proved. In Prague it is now called a lie. But a small group of collaborators may have helped the Soviets. On the afternoon of August 15, Party Secretary Indra, an ambitious, dangerous man, dismissed his personal staff at his office at the Central Committee Building. A girl secretary who had left something and returned, was surprised to see Indra sitting at the teleprinter. He got furious and threw her out but she had seen enough to know that he was in touch with Soviet Ambassador Cherwonenko.

Around midnight, on August 20, while Prague was asleep, Karel Hoffmann, Novotný's former Minister of Culture, whom Dubček later named director of the Office of the Administration of All Means of Communications (a rather unimportant job since Hoffmann was responsible only for technical problems, not policy decisions) gave orders to the engineers of the Prague Radio tower in nearby Český Brod to stop broadcasting. The Prague Radio was shut off when the Soviets took over the Prague Airport in Ruzyně.

How they did it, is already a legend of which several versions exist. An earlier version said that a civilian Aeroflot plane had asked the control tower for permission to land, and after stopping near the airport building, discharged a number of soldiers who jumped out and took over. Another version mentions a group of Intourist "travelers" who had arrived earlier and, under some pretext, were waiting at the transit room. A few minutes after 10 P.M., at a certain sign, they took, in perfect gangster style, submachine gun parts out of their briefcases, which they assembled. Then the "travelers," a special KGB commando, took over the airport.

Still another version exists which is confirmed by eyewitnesses. It begins at three minutes past 10 A.M., on August 20th, when red lights appeared in corridors and offices, and the phone rang in the office of the airport manager. He had just been about to go home. The last scheduled plane had arrived from Paris, and the next arrival would be the 5 A.M. Air India plane from New York on its way to New Delhi. The control tower asked the manager about an emergency call they'd just received from three Soviet transport planes that claimed to be short of fuel and asked for permission to land. The manager told the tower that the airport was closed, everybody had gone home. "Tell them to call the military airport of Kbely."

As the manager left his office, he heard the sound of a plane that had just set down on runway 25. He rushed to the nearest window. The plane reached the end of the runway, a second plane came down, and seconds later, a third plane. The doors

21

of the first plane opened, while the engines were still running, and black figures jumped out and ran toward the airport building. Almost instinctively, the manager pressed an alarm button and called into a microphone that was connected with the loudspeaker system: "The airport has been attacked! Switch off Velin!" "Velin" was the code name for the nerve center of Ruzyně Airport, regulating current, gas, water, heating, air conditioning. Only half a dozen people in Ruzyně knew about Velin.

Two seconds later the airport became completely dark. Some people had heard and executed the order. It was thirteen minutes past 10 P.M. Meanwhile more dark figures approached the airport, moving with strange dwarflike movements. Suddenly a searchlight turned on its beam against the airport building. The manager realized, horrified, that the "dwarfs" were Soviet parachutists wearing camouflage uniforms and steel helmets with red stars. Each of them had a machine around his neck. So that was it: the Soviets had landed. The emergency call had been a trick. There was no need to take over the military airport of Kbely. It had already fallen to the Russians by treason.

The Russian soldiers hurriedly installed more searchlights. They'd brought everything along—accumulators, cables, even a radar installation, and more lights. The manager remembers that within twenty minutes they had several lights set up near runway 25. More planes were now coming down, every minute one; it was a brilliantly executed operation. The planes were Antonow-12s and Antonow-22s. Some carried some armored vehicles, heavy guns, and heavy machine guns. The soldiers must have expected heavy resistance, for they approached the airport in attack formation.

But there was no resistance. The big question whether Czechoslovakia should have resisted will dominate people's thoughts for months, years, decades to come. The Czechoslovak leaders must have known since the ominous Dresden meeting in March 1968 that an intervention of the Warsaw

Pact was at least theoretically possible. When the Soviet tanks came, Czechoslovak Army officers looked on, with tears in their eyes, while hippies and minigirls attacked the tanks with their bare hands. Once before, the nation's leaders had decided to hand over their country with its well trained army, strong in morale and fighting power, without a shot. That was in 1938, at Munich, when the Czechoslovaks were not even consulted about their future. (In Warsaw, they were not consulted either, when the five Warsaw Pact powers wrote their "Dear Comrades" Letter.)

The Communists have called Edvard Beneš "a bourgeois weakling" and some have called him a "traitor." Beneš decided not to fight, hoping to save peace in our time. He only postponed the war for one year. Thirty years later, the Communist leaders made a similar decision. In both cases, the strategic situation of Czechoslovakia was equally desperate. In 1938, the country was completely surrounded by enemy powers. Not only Germany (and then German-associated Austria) but Hungary and Poland participated in the dismemberment of the country. The Czechs and Slovaks were told after Munich that the Soviets had not let them down— they hadn't taken part in the dismemberment. That is true; but they did occupy part of the country—Podkarpatská Rus, in 1945. Yet they didn't help the Czechoslovaks either, claiming they had no common frontier with Hitler-Germany.

Thirty years later, in 1968, the country was again surrounded by its hostile enemy brothers—the Soviet Cain, the DDR Cain, the Hungarian Cain, the Polish Cain. (Only the Bulgarian Cain had no common border with the Czechoslovak Republic.) Strategically, the country's position was more desperate even than in 1938. Only from the West, where a great part of the Czechoslovak Army was "guarding" the frontier against West Germany, "the revanchist arch-aggressor," according to Pravda, there was no danger. (The West German "aggressors" were the only ones that didn't think of an aggression.) The "fraternal" troops cut the country into ten strips. If the Czechoslovak Army had been ordered to resist, it would have been a short-lived resistance.

"But," says a Czech friend, "its memory might have lasted as long as the memory of the Greeks at Thermopylae, or of the Jews at Massada. It would have given our nation the moral strength that we will need in the years to come. We might have lost one generation of our men, but the nation might have gained much in return. "In the decisive phase we betrayed ourselves," wrote Ladislav Mňačko.

The Soviets calculated on strong Czechoslovak resistance. That was the real sense of the long summer maneuvers that didn't seem to end. The Soviets wanted to make sure that the Czechoslovak Army wasn't in positions where it might resist. But the possibility never arose. The government did not declare that a state of war existed between Czechoslovakia and the five "brother" countries.

The complete defeat of Czechoslovakia is only the first phase of the complete defeat of Soviet Communism. It is the end of an old pan-Slavistic myth, of strong pro-Soviet feelings in a country that was always traditionally pro-Russian. Soon the people of Czechoslovakia will hate the Soviets, as the people of Hungary, of Poland, of the DDR have long hated the Soviets. We've received letters from friends in Budapest, East Berlin and Warsaw telling us how shocked and desperate they were when they heard that their troops were ordered to take part "in this shameful execution." The love for the Soviet Union is gone—everywhere. The Kremlin has shown its true face as a brutal neocolonial power. The New Left in Europe, which accepted the occupation without an audible protest, now realizes that its naive belief in Castro and Ho Chi Minh is a fantasy. Both have approved of the occupation, and so have the Chinese who managed to both approve with the occupation and disagree with the Soviet Imperialists "that are not better than American Imperialists." The New Left has lost its decisive battle for the future, when it refused to speak up against a new form of leftist fascism.

The silence that followed the Soviet occupation will be heard all over the world for years and will haunt the United Nations. Just during the international year celebrating Human Rights, there occurred this brutal violation of Human Rights. U Thant, who was supposed to go to Prague, called off his visit, in order not to "interfere" with "internal" affairs of the Soviet bloc. *Cuius regio, eius religio.*

More Soviet planes were landing, while others took off again. The Soviets arrived in old American Dakota planes and Soviet Lichatchevs that had served in the Second World War. The Ruzyně Airport manager thought that around 11 P.M. several parachutist battalions had arrived in Ruzyně.

A few minutes past eleven, a Czechoslovak officer came into the manager's office. He wore a long leather coat and the insignia of an Air Force Colonel. He was Colonel Eliáš, chief pilot of ex-President Novotný. He told the manager to put "Velin" into action. The manager refused. Eliáš left, and the manager called the Prague police. But they couldn't help him. Soviet, East German, Hungarian, Polish and Bulgarian troops had invaded the country from thirteen different points. The manager was advised not to give any help to the occupiers. Then the phone went dead.

The manager put down the receiver. He heard how the entrance doors and windows were shattered. The Soviet soldiers were now inside the dark building. "They scurried around like rats, following their ratlike instincts" an eyewitness has said. "They plundered the duty-free shop. Within a few minutes, there wasn't a single bottle of Cognac or whiskey left there. Cigarettes, perfumes—everything disappeared. The Czechoslovak crew at the control tower had been thrown out by Eliáš and his men. But "Velin" wasn't working and none of the six persons who knew the secret gave it away. (It took the

Soviets three days to find "Velin" and put the nerve center into action.)

A Soviet officer came to see the manager. He asked whether the manager spoke Russian. The manager answered that he'd learned Russian in 1945, because he felt grateful to the Soviet liberators after the Nazi regime. The Soviet officer seemed embarrassed and said nothing. Then he asked the manager to go home. The manager and his people left the administration building and went to the parking lot. But their private cars had disappeared. And while they started walking the road toward Prague, several miles away, they saw how their cars were loaded into the empty Soviet planes.

At the same time, smaller planes carrying marine infantry and parachute units had landed on the new, unused autobahn in Spořilov, in southern Prague. By 2 A.M., people living near Lenin Street, that leads from Ruzyně Airport into Prague, were awakened by the noise of the tanks. Many turned on their radios; there was silence. Smrkovský later said, "Hoffmann is a traitor. He shut off our radio." Radio Prague resumed broadcasting only at 4:30 A.M. The tanks rode to the Square of the October Revolution in the suburb of Dejvice. From there, one column went south, toward Hradčany Castle, while another column went east, and later surrounded the office of the Prime Minister and the Central Committee Building. Still more tanks drove into the center of Prague, by way of Poříč, Příkopy, Wenceslas Square, toward the Prague Radio Building in Vinohradská.

As a military operation, it was all over. Czechoslovak Army experts now estimate that on the morning of August 21 not less than thirty divisions, seven thousand tanks, and more than one thousand planes were on Czechoslovak territory. Even if the Czechoslovak Army had put up resistance, it wouldn't have had the ghost of a chance. The troops of the Warsaw Pact Forces carried provisions only for three days when most of them were supposed to be withdrawn, after a Czechoslovak

26

"Revolutionary Workers' and Peasants' Government" had taken over the executive. This had been the political aim but it failed abysmally.

In the early morning hours, President Svoboda was informed that the "fraternal" troops had reached the outer courtyard of the Prague Castle. From the window of his residence the old general could see how the Presidential Guard was disarmed. A few shots were heard. Two early visitors came to see the President: Indra and Jozef Lennárt, the former Prime Minister under Novotný.

I'm told by a well-informed Party official, now a refugee in Vienna, that their meeting with Svoboda was short and dramatic.

"The President wore his dressing gown. He sat behind his desk, but he did not ask his visitors to sit down. Indra handed him a list of names: the new members of the "Revolutionary Workers' and Peasants' Government." Indra himself was supposed to be the new Prime Minister. A former Slovak journalist named Chnoupek was to be Interior Minister. Karel Hoffmann would again be Minister of Culture and Information. Other names on the list were Pavlovský, Novotný's former Ambassador in Moscow, Oldřich Švestka, still editor of *Rudé Pravo*, and František Barbírek. It is believed that Indra made up his list without even asking some of those he suggested.

"President Svoboda listened quietly. Then he shouted one word: 'Ven!' [out with you]. Even in his dressing gown he was still very much an Army General. Once more he shouted 'Ven!' and the traitors left."

Some people thought it was all over. But now it seems that it may have been only a beginning. It was something that hadn't happened to Bohemia since the Hussites fought against improbable odds five hundred years ago. The Hussites were not defeated by their enemies; they killed one another in the fratricidal battle of Lipány in 1434, when the conservative Utraquists and the radical Taborites exterminated each other.

(The events of the following weeks and months seem to prove that the descendants of the Hussites have learned the lesson of Lipány.) After a minute or so of silence, Radio Prague was on the air again with its regular theme song, the harp melody that is the beginning of Smetana's *My Country*. Then there was the sound of many confused voices and the woman announcer was back, introducing Alois Poledňiák, vice-president of the National Assembly. He didn't sound afraid; he made a short speech, comparing this day to March 15, 1939, when the Nazi troops moved in, and asking the people to remain calm. There was more shooting, and people booing and shouting. (At that time, we learned later, the Soviet troops clashed first with their improbable antagonists—girls in miniskirts and blue-jeaned boys in Beatle haircuts. They formed a barricade in front of the radio building, and sat down in the street as the tanks advanced. The defensive force held firm, and the tanks came to a stop. Somebody was waving the Czechoslovak flag, with the red-white-blue colors of the American and French flags. Bulldozers, bakers' delivery trucks and streetcars formed a barricade at the corner of Vinohradská and Italská Streets.)

A few minutes later a man's voice said this was Radio Gottwaldov (the former town of Zlín, headquarters of the Baťa [now Svit] shoe factories). "We too may be silenced soon," he said. "People just phoned that a tank column is moving up here. Friends, let's all stick together from now on. This time there must be no collaborators, no meanness, no opportunism, no stupidity." For the first time a Czechoslovak radio station addressed its audience not as "comrades" or "citizens," but as "friends." They were all friends now; only Party officials occasionally talked to their "comrades"; a habit is hard to break. The man warned against provocateurs, and asked people to phone Gottwaldov 66-51 if they saw any troop movements. "Make banners and posters in *azbuka* (Cyrillic letters). Tell the Russians to go home; they are uninvited guests. Keep away from them. . . ." I heard angry shouts, booing, whistling (a sound of disapproval here). The man continued calmly,

"Friends, to oppose them by force would be stupid suicide. Our only weapon now is absolute, complete passive resistance. I was in Prague when the Nazis came in 1939 and I cried, but today I'm too deeply hurt, too angry to cry. This morning, our so-called friends are shooting at our people. No fatalism, friends, no capitulation—but no idiocy either. . . . I just hear there'll be a two-minute silence at noon. Not more than two minutes, and discipline, please."

An announcer said, "This is the free, legal [*svobodné, legální*] Czechoslovak radio." It was the first indication that a free, clandestine network had been set up. Another voice came on: "In the next few days we'll have to show political maturity and national strength. The whole world must know that the people are united as never before. Our actions must be dignified, never primitive." A woman said that the young children in nearby "pioneer" summer camps were all right, and that parents shouldn't worry. She stammered a little as she spoke and apologized. "It's not easy to speak when you know the whole country is listening. Please phone us exact news. Be specific. Give exact data, names, localities. . . . We have tried to get in touch with Prague but they don't answer. Remember, friends—we are with you, be with us!" (*"Jsme s Vámi, bud'te s námi"* became the great slogan of the resistance.) After a while a man said they had a great many calls and were happy to be in touch with their listeners. He asked people who listened in to tell students near the theater not to do anything foolish. . . . "We hear that lists of signatures are prepared demanding the instantaneous departure of the occupiers—" Somebody interrupted him, "We've got Prague!" And then a woman said, "This is the free, legal Czechoslovak radio in Prague. . . ."

During much of the following week I stayed close to my radio in Vienna, day and night, monitoring the story of the Czechoslovak reaction to the Soviet invasion. It isn't the complete story of the resistance, of course. It would have taken several people and better equipment than I had to follow the transmissions of the clandestine network, which would often switch frequencies, as its stations moved with bewildering speed from one place to another. In the beginning, the voices on the air simply tried to give people moral support, but gradually they came to direct resistance activities, and finally took over the job of running a country that had no government for a whole week. The studios of all the official stations were soon occupied. The last one, Radio Budweis (České Budějovice) reported at 5:04 A.M. on August 23 that it was being surrounded. By that time, the network was functioning all over the country, from the Bohemian Forest along Czechoslovakia's Bavarian border, to the lonely mountains in eastern Slovakia, near the Soviet frontier. There were well-known radio voices and also voices that one had never heard before. The microphones picked up strange background noises, creaking doors being opened and closed (attic? cellar? stable?), people carrying on a discussion in a nearby room, somebody shouting a warning or asking for coffee. Someday the saga of the secret network will be written by one who worked for it—a great story of courage and cunning, primitive help—yourself and ingenious skill. Even under normal conditions, radio stations in Czechoslovakia had not always been models of efficiency. There would be sudden breakdowns, technical troubles followed by embarrassed explanations, power shortages. Equipment failed and cables broke down.

And now, the master technicians managed to put together an entire new network under the most difficult conditions, surrounded by half a million soldiers, many of whom were looking for them. Sometimes as many as nineteen stations were operating a *štafeta* (relay program). Each station was allotted nine minutes, and a central station, probably near Prague, would regulate the flow of news and occasionally interrupt with important, life-or-death bulletins. ("Friends in České Budějovice, take your belongings and run, they're coming!") The central station would organize the sequence, giving priority to stations with emergency status. Now and then, one would complain that it was not being well treated, and then Prague would tell it to be reasonable, and remind it that the national interest was more important than any regional one. Gradually, the Slovak stations gained equal time, and status, with those in Bohemia and Moravia, as it became clear that the Slovaks would not break away, as many people had feared. In the hour of crisis, the Slovaks reaffirmed their common destiny with the Czechs, putting aside all past resentments.

Every few minutes, an announcer would repeat that this was a "free, legitimate station," to make it clear to the people who had just tuned in, that it was not one run by the Russians. The network broadcast on a twenty-four-hour schedule. Sometimes the voices grew hoarse with fatigue, but the spirit remained unbroken. A station might disappear but then two new ones would join the chorus. Probably several hundred people were involved—writers, editors, reporters, announcers, technicians, messengers—and they were aided by a legion of volunteers who phoned or sent messages, brought food, fooled the occupiers. (Travelers saw a great many motorcycle riders all over the country, some of them carrying fishing gear, though no one was seen fishing.)

Gradually the network became consolidated, gave weather reports for the farmers, issued orders to the citizens, delivered important messages all over the country when all other communications had broken down. The whole country kept in touch by way of the invisible network; everybody knew what was going on elsewhere. Under the pressure of time, mistakes were bound to happen. Not every bit of news could be carefully checked, and there were denials and apologies. The resistance from the air was characterized by passion and dignity, and by a typically Czechoslovak mixture of idealism with practical methods. The resistance has changed the image of Hašek's Schweik, who outsmarted authority by playing dumb. The radio and TV Schweiks, anno 1968, were intelligent people fighting with words against guns, with dignity against

31

violence. "Long after the crimes of the Stalins and Brezhnevs will be forgotten, our short-lived resistance will be remembered in the history books," a Czech friend says.

The Soviets were infuriated and finally demoralized by the unseen voices that kept up the great fight, day and night. They shot at power stations and transmitters, destroyed some studios, cut cables. Yet the voices were still there, talking without hatred but sometimes with biting irony. The Soviet-controlled Vltava (Moldau) station was quickly discredited by the underground stations, which obligingly broadcast Vltava's wavelength, and told people to listen to it for amusement. "It's interesting to hear them talk about how they protect our Socialism and give us fraternal help while a tank is driving up in front of your house and shooting your windows out," a man said. Vlatava's very language would give it away: the occupiers became "our united armies," aggression was called "protective measures," the invasion turned into "peace offensive," and patriotism was, of course, "counterrevolution." Often the announcers couldn't even speak correct Czech or Slovak.

The entire population was listening to the clandestine network. Many people knew where the nearest station at the moment happened to be. Old ladies brought the workers flowers and cookies, telling a Soviet patrol to look for them in the opposite direction. There were stations that stayed in one place and also mobile ones, many, it seemed, under control of the Czechoslovak Army. Most stations would automatically get silent when they were touched by electronic locating equipment. Large enterprises—the Tesla plants manufacturing electronic equipment; the Česká Loděnice shipyards which have been working on contracts for the Soviet Union; Českomoravská-Kolben-Daněk, a large machine factory; and quite a few others—had their own transmitters, which were used by the technicians both for the transmission of news and to jam the Russian stations. (Russian army commanders complained bitterly that they were out of touch with other units.) Thus the destruction of many transmitters could not disrupt

32

the network. Still, skilled improvisation alone couldn't have kept the stations going for over a week. The state postal administration (which runs telephone and telegraph service normally) was in on the job, and so were special army units, technicians and radio hams. Heinrich Böll, the West German novelist, who happened to be in Prague during the resistance, was asked by Czech writer friends to make a statement for the free radio. "We went to a nearby apartment, I spoke into the phone, and a little later they heard me all over the country," he said.

Jindřich Popelka, chief editor of the Brno, Moravia, television, who got to Vienna after Soviet General I. Pavlovsky threatened "to level the city" if the infernal radio and TV business wouldn't stop, told a friend, "The Soviets often drove past our emergency studios but they couldn't find us. While we were on the air the first day, our technicians built three provisional studios out of the equipment of one small station. At one point, our studio was in an office, and from there we went to a factory. After ten minutes on the air, we would go off for five minutes to work on the latest news. We slept little, every night in a different place—in the homes of friends or of people we'd never known before. We were one big family. The secret network operated so beautifully because it was supported by fourteen million friends." Popelka later returned to Brno.

By noontime on the day of the invasion, the "free, legitimate" station in Prague was broadcasting reports from all over the country. Instructions were given how to confuse the occupiers. "Switch around street signs and highway markers, paste arrows with the word MOCKBA (Moscow) on top of road signs, write banners with the words *Eto naše dielo* (This is our affair)." This was a reference to Brezhnev's words, "Comrades, this is your affair," spoken when he was in Prague shortly before Novotný was ousted, and he was asked to mediate. Trenčín, Slovakia, reported that Dubček's mother was worried about her son—if anyone had news, would he please get in

33

touch with her? (The Soviets, who had news, didn't tell her that her son had been handcuffed and taken like a criminal to the Ruzyně Airport from where he was flown by Soviet jet to Lwów and later to Moscow.) The newly elected delegates of the Fourteenth Party Congress were told to go to Prague "at once, and by all possible means." The Congress had originally been called for September 9 to elect a new Central Committee which every one expected to be overwhelmingly pro-Dubček, and many observers in Prague believe that the Soviets decided to intervene to forestall preparations for the Party Congress. The delegates were told *not* to report to Congress headquarters at the Hotel Praha. (Ten minutes later, big signs went up in Příkopy, near the entrance of Hotel Praha, warning everybody that there were spies inside the hotel.) Instead they were told to report to Party district offices and big factories for instructions. Some delegates went by bicycles, others were hidden in delivery trucks or in factory ambulances, to fool the Soviet soldiers who had cut off all roads leading to Prague.

The "free, legitimate" Ostrava Radio reported that the two-minute-silence demonstration had come off well. People were told to tune in their radios either on middle wave 470, Prague, or long wave 1103, Brno. Messages of support for Dubček reached all stations. The Czechoslovak Army was standing loyally behind President Svoboda. Prague broadcast a short dialogue from Wenceslas Square, between a Czech student and two Soviet soldiers. The student asked, "Why do you shoot at us? We are Socialists, like you." The soldiers said *nyet*, they were shooting at Western imperialists. End of the dialogue. The free, legal Bratislava station proclaimed the solidarity of Slovaks and Czechs. (A few days earlier, a friend in Prague had said, "Bratislava is three hundred kilometers away from Prague and three hundred years behind it.") Vasil Bilák, the Slovak Communist Party boss, was called "a traitor."

Late in the afternoon, the situation got tense and there were many appeals to keep calm. A spokesman of the Writers' Union asked people "to use the weapons of the mind," and said there must be no Budapest, that's just what *"they"* would want. A voice interrupted, warning the people in Prague to leave the streets around the Prague radio station in Vinohrady immediately, the Soviet tanks were firing there. "We beg you all to get off the streets," a woman said. (In critical moments, women announcers were used, perhaps on the theory that their emotional impact was stronger than men's.)

The first appeals were made to the world at large. Spokesmen for Czechoslovakia's doctors, writers, engineers, artists, addressed their colleagues everywhere on earth "to help their fight for humanity and freedom." A man spoke in Russian to the Soviet soldiers, "Friends (if I may still call you that), in this country there are no counterrevolutionaries. Socialism is not endangered. You've seen our beautiful country. . . . How would you feel if occupying troops suddenly came into your country? . . . Please go home before it is too late."

Somebody said he'd seen Czech boys and girls hold their transistor radios up to the tanks so the Soviets could hear the Russian broadcast. "We must not blame the soldiers, one commentator said. . . . They have their orders. Explain the situation to them, simply and clearly, explain what Dubček has done to make the Communist Party truly representative of the nation."

Bad news: Party Secretary Čestmír Cisář, whom the ideologists of Moscow's *Pravda* had called a heretic, had been seen taken into Prague police headquarters on Bartolomějská Street. Somebody read a poem by Josef Hora. In the Vinohrady district, Russian tanks had brutally smashed parked automobiles and knocked down some beautiful old trees. They had also ruined the pavement of Nerudova Street, leading up to the Prague Castle. ("Many of them were old T-34 tanks that had been in Prague during the Liberation, in May 1945. . . . What a terrible irony!") At Hradčany Castle, the government was in session, "attended by all ministers able to get there." Another appeal in Russian was read to the Soviet soldiers, reminding them of June 22, 1939, when Hitler's Wehrmacht had suddenly invaded the Soviet Union, in violation of the Molotov-Ribbentrop non-aggression Pact, or perhaps because of it. "Those among your officers old enough to remember can imagine how we feel today. . . . It would be a tragic mistake if your brutal intervention would end forever our twenty-three-year-old friendship."

Listeners were told what had happened in the early-morning hours, when the Soviets had surrounded the Central Committee Building overlooking the Moldau and had arrested several Presidium members in Dubček's office. Hradčany Castle, Černín Palace (the Ministry of Foreign Affairs, from which Jan Masaryk had mysteriously fallen to his death in 1948) and the Interior Ministry were completely surrounded by Soviet tanks. The investigation into the circumstances of Jan Masaryk's death, which had started months ago and had been scheduled to continue until the end of the year, was off, for the time being; the Soviet secret police was said to have been involved. And a recording featuring a speech by President T. G. Masaryk that had been prepared in celebration of the fiftieth anniversary of the Republic, on October 28, would not be issued. . . .

A woman announcer reported that Soviet soldiers had killed four workers in Prague. Her voice was trembling. Some streetcars were running. All railroad stations were occupied, and no trains had arrived or left for hours. Around Prague-Střed (Center) railroad station, which elderly streetcar conductors had again called "Masaryk Station" in the past months, the Soviets had posted tanks, rockets and antiaircraft guns, for reasons known only to themselves. Three houses in Vinohrady, near the Prague Radio building, were damaged and one was burning. Many delegates to the Party Congress "had reached their destination." (Later, we heard that the Congress took place in a big hall of the Českomoravská-Kolben-Danek machine factory in Prague. Many delegates had been smuggled in wearing workers' overalls and carrying workers' identification cards. In the vicinity, three "simulated" Congresses were held to confuse the Soviets, who couldn't locate the Congress, which was attended by almost eleven hundred out of the elected fifteen hundred delegates.)

People were warned not to take pictures while they were observed by the Soviets, who would "confiscate" cameras and tape recorders. At 8 P.M. Radio Gottwaldov came on the air. The Communist Party district leader, introduced by name, said that Gottwaldov had become "a dead city." "Ignore them," he said. "Keep your doors and windows closed. . . . We must make a difference between the Soviet leadership and the Russian people. A Russian girl, who works here, will speak to you now." I heard a soft, shaken Russian voice. The girl said she was terrified; she was convinced that most soldiers didn't know where they were and why they were here. "I was so happy when I saw Comrades Brezhnev and Dubček on television, embracing each other. . . . I hope with all my heart that someday you will forget what happened here, but I am afraid, yes, I know, that the feelings between our two nations will never be as before. . . ."

The National Assembly, in permanent session in its temporary headquarters on Jindřišská Street, issued a strong proclamation. The invasion had grossly violated international law, it said; all interned Czechoslovak leaders must be released at once; all occupation troops must leave instantly; the citizens were asked not to let themselves provoke the invaders. "If necessary, the last means of resistance will be a general strike." It was the strongest statement issued so far, although the deputies in the Assembly meeting were virtual prisoners, surrounded by Soviet tanks.

At 4:30 P.M., Prague reported the Writers' Union building in Národní Třída had been occupied. A man said, "This is our last message to you, friends. Remember, we are all together now; there are no differences of origin, language, religion, race. More than ever we are aware of our historical mission in the fight for truth and freedom. . . . Keep up the fight! Don't ever give in! Do only what has to be done. Help us to protect the sovereignty of our country."

An announcer asked people near Soviet tanks to hold up their radios to the Soviet soldiers, they would repeat the message from the Russian girl. Later a Polish woman was introduced "who came to our studio voluntarily." She started reading from a script but then she became carried away and made a moving improvised appeal to the Polish troops, reminding them of her country's great past, "the centuries-old fight of our people against the Russians. . . ." She had to break off, overcome by tears. (Later that evening I heard another Polish woman praising the "historical friendship of the Czechoslovak and Polish brother nations," their fight side by side against the Nazis during the Second World War, "the blood shed by the Second Polish Army during the Liberation of Slovakia." Then Chopin's "Revolutionary Etude" was played, and a voice said, "This is the Czech-language program of Radio Warsaw.")

At 5:15 P.M. Gottwaldov was on the air again, "broadcasting from a substitute studio." The announcer said the streets were empty and the squares were silent; yes, Gottwaldov had become a dead city, and the occupiers didn't know where to turn. No one sold the Soviets any food. He warned especially "our dear old mothers" (*maminky*) to give the soldiers "not even a pitcher of milk." Radio Brno interrupted with an important message. "Strange men with forged Czechoslovak identity cards are going around, trying to make arrests. Please notify our police if you see anything suspicious."

The editors of *Literární Listy* greeted the people "in this hour of our worst ordeal" (*nejvyšší nouze*) and announced a special edition that was now being distributed. They asked everybody to join them "in the fight for the truth to the bitter end." Another man warned journalists and printers not to publish anything that had been censored. The lawyers' association appealed to jurists all over the world "to help in this struggle for legality, humanity, freedom." A woman announcer said they were getting so many messages that it was impossible to broadcast them all. Prague switched to Plzeň where a Czech read a thickly accented, very effective appeal in English. A local Party official reported on his delegation's negotiations with the Soviet commander in Pilsen.

The general said it was all a misunderstanding that would soon be cleared up. We asked him why his government sent troops to the workers' city of Pilsen. He said they were here to protect us against imminent danger from the West German Bundeswehr. That left us speechless. The general looked confused and said he hoped to have more information later on. We demanded that normal conditions be guaranteed in Pilsen, that communications must be kept functioning, and we said we shall not tolerate more than a minimum movement of troops. He said he would comply provided there were no incidents. We emphatically repeated there was no reason why Soviet troops should interfere.

Radio České Budějevice introduced itself with a short Russian appeal to the troops. ("Can you imagine that the Chinese would invade the Soviet Union in order to protect you? . . . Go home, soldiers. Your country will soon need you more than ours.") At 7:50 P.M. Prague sent an appeal of the Czechoslovak youth to young people everywhere. Some baroque music (Vivaldi?) was played. Blood donors were urgently needed. A man asked people "to stay at home during this long, hard night." Jiří Dienstbier, a well-known commentator, warned against rumors. "We are not in touch with our government leaders. . . . But we want to make it absolutely clear that no one asked these troops to come here. This isn't Budapest. A delegation of our deputies went to the Soviet Embassy to demand the withdrawal of the troops. The delegation has not returned. . . ." Another commentator followed:

In this country, we have a long experience with occupiers. We have been occupied for centuries. Friends, this time we're going to need all our experience. Yesterday's brothers became today's enemies. They don't understand what they are doing here. Will anyone be willing to form an occupation regime? So far they were unable to find such people. They badly misjudged the situation. They may say *veni, vidi* but not *vici*. . . . I do hope that no traitor, collaborationist, careerist will betray Dubček. Trust in yourselves and we trust you. . . .

Then Jiří Hejzlar, director of the Czechoslovak radio, was introduced. (He has since been dismissed at the insistence of the Soviets.)

Dear friends . . . Our history is a history of unhappiness. This is one of the saddest days of all. . . . Friends, our weapon is our dignity. Outside, it's getting dark but the tragic day isn't over yet. We cannot answer all questions and messages but do trust us: we stand firmly behind Dubček and Svoboda. We shall be on the air all night long, and if they silence us, we'll broadcast from elsewhere. Beware of provocateurs and adventurers trying to spread poison and panic. Be careful and be watchful. . . . We are with you; be with us.

An announcer said they were now broadcasting over three medium wavelengths—233 meters, 428 meters, 492 meters, and over long wave at 1103 meters. The secret network was getting organized.

The morning broadcast, on Thursday, August 22, of Radio Austria transmitted a telephone conversation between its correspondent in Linz and an editor of Radio České Budějovice. ("Don't worry about us, Fritz. They won't get us. They cannot search every house, every stable, every attic. . . . If we get suddenly silent, you will hear from us again after some time.") Brno asked everybody "to collect pictures, documents and other material for future use to prove even to the most cynical observer that we wanted nothing but our own, democratic Socialism—and what our former friends did to us." For the first time, Drahomír Kolder, Vasil Bilák, Alois Indra and František Barbirek were called "traitors and collaborationists." Prague had a new station signal, a dark, forbidding, foghorn-like sound. A woman announced that the bakers had worked all night as usual, and there was enough fresh bread. An anonymous guitarist sang his new song, *"Pravda je s námi,"* ("The truth is with us/ If you hold out/ The world will again be ours.") Ostrava reported growing tension. During the night, an old man with a heart attack was taken by ambulance to the hospital. The Soviets had refused to let the ambulance go through. The old man was smuggled to the hospital in a vegetable truck. He was getting better. Brno announced a television program from a secret studio, *držte nám palce,* keep your fingers crossed. People were asked to write the Russian word *Pochemoo* (Why?) on Soviet tanks. "In the streets of Prague there is shooting. You can well imagine who is shooting." One free station thanked the people for sending food and offering "to take care of our kids while we are here."

People were told how to behave toward collaborators. "You know nothing, you say nothing, you don't betray, and, above all, *you won't forget.* . . . Our position is clear. Who is not with us is against us. Remember, the real counterrevolutionaries sit in their tanks. *They* have betrayed Socialism." Prague said that some food rationing might be necessary. The people of Gottwaldov demanded the recall of Alois Indra, National Assembly deputy for Gottwaldov. "To recall the traitor, we ask you to sign your name and address, and add the stamp of your organization, to make such documents valid and legal. . . . Let me add a few personal words. On my way to the studio I saw big signs, 'Death to Traitors.' Friends, let's remain decent, in spite of everything. We wish death to no one. We must not betray our sacred hope by acting as *they* do. . . ." Prague read a commentary that reminded me of some recent articles in *Literární Listy.* Probably it had been written by a member of the staff.

. . . we must simply accept the truism that the whole history of mankind is a perpetual fight for freedom. We tried to do our bit in this fight but now we've been taken over by the powers of darkness. But even a man without arms is not unarmed. No one can take away our honor and our dignity. For the time being you can still hear us. And if we should become silent, remember Jan Werich's song "See you again in better times. . . ."

Prague said that members of the KGB (the Soviet secret police) had arrived in town and were trying to arrest members of the Communist Party. At eight in the morning a sniper had fired a shot from a window near the Palacký bridge in Smíchov, whereupon Soviet tanks had retaliated by shooting out the windows in several houses. People were warned not to do such foolish things. Gasoline would have to be rationed. Radio Gottwaldov demanded that Dubček appear on television until eight that night, otherwise there should be a two-hour general strike. "We suggest an ultimatum." The Brno studio was in danger; people were asked not to use certain telephone numbers which were tapped. The Organization of Czechoslovak Mothers appealed to the Russian mothers whose sons were among the occupation troops to demand their recall. "There is no reason why they should be here." The Brno post office no longer accepted telegrams. It was suggested to give them to people leaving the city. All radio amateurs were asked to jam the programs of the Russian "Vltava" station. Brno said that a traitor had told the Soviets the address of their studio and gave an exact description of the man. "The Soviets have just entered the back yard," the announcer said calmly. One heard shouts of "Hanba!" (shame) and "Ať žije Dubček! [Long live Dubček!]." The announcer, now somewhat breathless, expressed regrets for running away now, and reminded people there would be a one-hour general strike at noon. Then there was a violent noise, tables and chairs turned over, loud voices—and

42

suddenly silence. What was happening? Had the man whose voice we'd just heard been arrested? Or worse?

A few seconds later, Brno was on the air again. Another announcer said, cheerfully, "Well, friends, here we are again, from another studio." A Czech poem was read, possibly to gain time, since the news service hadn't been set up yet, but the station must not remain silent. People had become so used to the voices from the ether that any protracted silence created fear.

The announcer apologized for certain technical difficulties, "but our men are doing all they can." A new wave length was given. Milk bottles were urgently needed, though there was enough milk. Don't put your signature on sheets of white paper with no text; such lists might be used by provocateurs. Ostrava announced that all local newspapers had appeared this morning under one masthead to simplify difficult operations. A member of the Moravian Writers' Union said, "We listen to the conscience of the world but all we hear is silence. The big powers have only their big-power interests. . . . What happens here made a caricature of Leninism. Still, we remain faithful to the ideals of *our* Socialism and will never collaborate with quislings. There is no time for long speeches but there will be plenty of time for long memories. . . ."

The announcer said that all Party Congress delegates from Brno had arrived in Prague. "If you can hear us, Prague, tell our delegates we are with them." The Parliamentarian delegation had not yet returned from the Soviet Embassy and had probably been arrested. A man said, "Folks, did you hear the latest one? What will these Soviet soldiers tell their friends when they return to Russia? Answer: nothing, because they'll all be sent to prison."

A member of the Central Committee, who apologized for not giving his name, told the people what had happened in Dubček's office during the night of the invasion. The Presidium had been in session, as every Tuesday night, and the Soviets knew where to find most of the Czechoslovak leaders. Prime

Minister Černik had received a call from a Czechoslovak officer that the invasion had started. (The report has since been published everywhere.) The speaker said that at least three men present—Bilák, Kolder, Indra—seemed unsurprised by the news, and he continued:

> It is perhaps not unfair to assume that they had known about it. Dubček said, with tears in his eyes, "How could they do this to me? . . . This is the tragedy of my life." He had just read a letter from Brezhnev, written the day before, that made no mention of the invasion. Two days earlier, he'd met secretly his old friend Kadar, who told him nothing about the intervention that was then being prepared. . . . At one-thirty, after the announcement was given to the radio and the papers, some people left. Dubček and Kriegel stayed, Smrkovský went to the National Assembly to convene an emergency session. Černik went to his office, which was already occupied. . . . (Pause) When I left the Central Committee Building, the tanks had arrived but I managed to get away. . . . And that, friends, is how the betrayal was carried out. I've told you this secret report so you will all know the truth. . . . Thank you, friends.

Dubček, Smrkovský and Kriegel were arrested in Dubček's office, by Soviet secret police, acting "in the name of the Revolutionary Workers' and Peasants' Government of Comrade Indra." Prime Minister Černik was arrested at his office and handcuffed. They were first taken in armored cars to Warsaw and flown to Mukačevo (which once was part of Czechoslovakia and in 1945 annexed by the Soviets).

At a recent meeting between Dubček and Černik, and the presidents of the Czechoslovak universities, Dubček was asked, "Did you know that the Soviets were going to invade Czechoslovakia?" Dubček said, "We all knew it might happen but I personally just couldn't believe it." Černik agreed. Interior Minister Pavel seemed to have lost his nerve and was hiding from August 21 until August 23; later he offered his resignation which was accepted by Svoboda. Four deputy Interior Ministers were arrested by the Soviets. A fifth, named Zaruba, shot himself in his office, refusing to collaborate with the KGB.

Villiam Šalgovič, repeatedly called a traitor by the free radio stations, collaborated with the Soviet secret police. He was to arrange for a coordination of the Czechoslovak secret police with the KGB but the Czechoslovak police, from traffic cop up to the highest officers, did not collaborate. The patriotic, decent behavior of the Czechoslovak police forces is unique in the history of Communist police forces, which is not often a nice one. Czechoslovak secret police helped to distribute underground newspapers and in many cases saved journalists and radio technicians from Soviet commando forces. (Šalgovič is now in Moscow in exile.)

Indra who had gone to Moscow with the Czechoslovak delegation suffered a heart attack, and returned to Prague only on September 27. Kolder remained at the Central Committee Building, after Dubček, Smrkovský and Kriegel had been arrested. It is reliably reported that some of Kolder's henchmen addressed him at once, "Comrade First Secretary." After the return of the Czechoslovak delegation from Moscow, Kolder left the country. He is said to be in Sofia, perhaps waiting for a summons.

Yet some members of Novotný's Old Stalinist Guard have surprised everybody. Novotný himself, perhaps disappointed because Moscow didn't call him, remains in Prague and has said that he had "nothing to do" with the occupation. Most people believe this. His former Minister of Defense, General Lomský, an old Moscow-trained *apparachik* who had been deposed by the Dubček regime but remained a deputy of the National Assembly, stayed at the Assembly Building during the first days. The building was surrounded by Soviet tanks. Lomský, who speaks perfect Russian, on several occasions angrily argued with the Soviet officers. Showing his uniforms with many Soviet decorations, he dared them to enter the building. It is said in Prague that Lomský during the seven days after the invasion "made up for his sins during the past seven years." Another once pro-Russian deputy, General Kodaj, who had created much excitement when he called "Two Thousand Words" a "counterrevolutionary appeal," after August 21 atoned by publicly asking that "war should be declared on the Soviet Union." Such statements show the enormous scope of the Kremlin's political failure. With very, very few exceptions, there were no traitors. Even those once pro-Soviet Czechoslovaks on whom Moscow counted, refused to collaborate.

My friend J. wrote me late in September:

> The press and radio refuse to publish lies about "counter-revolutionaries"—on the contrary, with government and Party backing, they deny these lies and protest against them. This puts the Soviets in a dilemma: either they'll have to wipe out the whole nation the way Stalin dealt with subjugated peoples or they have to accept their political and moral defeat and try to keep up the pressure. The risks are high but it seems that the people in Prague have decided there is no other way. The leaders refuse to corrupt their own people and rather face the possibility of total annihilation . . . Even a Soviet purge would not change too much under the circumstances. It would only mean a change of persons, not of ideas and attitudes. This, then, is the optimistic outlook . . . The pessimistic would be reoccupation, military government, a "protectorate" or inclusion in the U.S.S.R.

In Czechoslovakia, the national heroes range from great humanists—Comenius, Hus, Masaryk—to famous ice-hockey players, but there were almost no generals and politicians among them. Paradoxically, Alexander Dubček, the son of a Communist and himself always a Communist who was not long ago an unknown *apparachik*, became within a few months a national hero among the overwhelmingly non-Communist population. Back in 1957, Antonin Novotný had called Dubček, then a student at the Party Cadre College in Moscow, "one of the best, who will go far in our Party." Dubček went farther than Novotný may have wished. There is nothing heroic about this frail man with the face of a melancholy clown whom his countrymen compare to Jan Hus and Martin Luther. Dubček was said to dislike such comparisons, as he disliked the trappings of power. In the city of Franz Kafka, Dubček successfully practiced the cult of un-personality. Yet he introduced an element of style into Communist politics, where style is considered a bourgeois aberration.

Some people in Prague said that Dubček reminded them of John F. Kennedy. There is no external similarity between the two men, but the comparison wasn't altogether wrong. Dubček projected an image and he gave people a vision. He didn't bring his style to his mission, though; it was the mission that formed his political style. T. G. Masaryk used to say that democracy was discussion; Dubček defined democracy as a clash of views. "Democracy," he once said, "is also conscientious discipline and calls for statesmanlike wisdom of all citizens." The emphasis was on "all," which irritated the Soviets. In the Kremlin's view, the Communist Party remains an elite that keeps its distance from "all" citizens. The Soviets, pathologically distrustful as ever, found it inconceivable that the population at large should line up behind Dubček. They didn't believe it. They suspected a gigantic conspiracy.

The Soviet leaders, as all doctrinaire believers, were always afraid of their own disciples who might develop the evolution of the doctrine. (Who can tell where the border line is between evolution and counterrevolution? At the Philosophical Congress in Vienna, early in September, Professor Konstantinov, a Soviet philosopher, claimed exclusive rights to Marxist philosophy and called the intervention in Czechoslovakia "a service to peace in Europe," whereupon Professor Klibansky, Canada, noted that philosophers such as Konstantinov consider all dissenters as "either scoundrels or fools.")

The Soviet leaders, as all doctrinaire believers, were always father was one of the earliest members, since 1925, of the Czechoslovak Communist Party. Dubček, a worker (engine-fitter), had studied in the Soviet Union, later joined the Slovak Partisans in their fight against the Germans. After he became First Party Secretary last January, it took him some time to get through to the people. He was a colorless man and a dull speaker. Yet he fascinated millions of television viewers, even foreigners who didn't understand him. People instinctively sensed his honesty and warmth, his modesty and humanity. They felt that he was one of them, after listening for thirty years to political dictators and cynical demagogues. He treated people as human beings, thanked them for their support. They were no longer faceless members of a crowd; he spoke to each of them. *Reportér,* until the invasion the newsweekly of the Journalists' Union, wrote, "For the first time in thirty years, for the first time in the life of a generation, we are again proud to be Czechs and Slovaks. . . . Those of us who are members of the Communist Party can after a long time again walk upright and look people in the eyes. We are no longer prison guards and are again citizens. . . . Our friends abroad should tell us whether they want to remain our friends or prison guards. We've had enough guards until now, but never enough friends." The "friends," alas, have since told them the answer. My friend J., the amateur historian, on my last day in Prague summed it up. "Dubček is always completely himself; that is his strength and may be his weakness. He is just as relaxed among workers as among intellectuals. Look at the way he dresses! He doesn't feel he has to demonstrate his Marxist *Weltanschauung* by a tieless shirt and a crumpled suit. He is what you in America call a swell guy, which cannot be said of many contemporary statesmen on both sides of the Iron Curtain."

"Somebody must have spoken ill of Josef K., for, without having done anything bad, he was arrested one morning," Kafka writes in the beginning of *The Trial.* Perhaps the trial of Alexander D. is only beginning.

Radio Prague asked people who had tape recorders to record the speech of the Central Committee member that would soon be repeated, "because we must destroy our own material." A Czechoslovak army colonel asked all citizens to avoid incidents and to give "our former allies" no help whatsoever. In Brno, people were urged to leave the streets and go home immediately. "This is the free, legal radio, citizens," said the woman announcer. "It is no trick. Go home, please, and the tanks will move out of the center of the city." A guitarist sang another song, and the woman came on again to thank the listeners for their support and sympathy. "We don't feel heroic at all, just a little tired," she said. "We are doing our job, don't feel sorry for us. Once more, please go home, especially you people standing around in Náměstí Svobody (Freedom Square)." She turned away from the microphone and talked to a man. They had forgotten they were on the air, and everybody could listen in on their private conversation. He said that he'd brought her a message, and that he was glad to meet her in person, after hearing her on the air for the past two days. She laughed.

He said, "You are too young to remember what happened in 1939. I didn't realize you would be so young. And so pretty." Somebody in the background shouted something, and the girl drew in her breath, and said, "Goodness, I didn't know, we were on the air," and then she began to read the message, in her official-sounding voice. I hope everybody enjoyed the little interlude as I did. Radio Budějovice was on. A man said all was quiet for a change, on the house walls signs had appeared saying U.S.S.R. = S.S. (In France last summer, I saw signs, U.S. = S.S., with references to Vietnam.) A father of two boys asked them to come home. The announcer added, "Yes, parents, tell all your boys and girls not to run around the tanks, it's dangerous. . . . And now to Prague." A woman announcer asked radio amateurs in eastern Slovakia to listen over the 800-meter wave length and spread the news until better connections could be established. Suddenly a voice shouted, "This is Hradec Králové, get away from that burning tank, people, don't stand around! They may shoot!" Then a calm voice, from another station, read a news bulletin. In Belgrade, 250,000 people had attended a protest meeting. Young people in Prague were warned not to mill around Wenceslas Square, and then Budějovice was on again, telling people an allegory. "Christ had only one Judas but we have five."

At six in the morning, on Friday, August 23, Radio Ostrava reported that the free, legal radio was consolidating its operations. The occupied ones had better nerves than their occupiers. People were going to work everywhere, as usual. In Prague, many newspapers had been secretly printed during the night and were now being distributed. In Plzeň, the local *Pravda* had come out in a legal edition, with a codework. There was also a Russian-edited edition which people were asked to ignore. They were also told not to sell the Soviets any food, "unless they force you at gun point." Messages were welcomed, but they must have names and addresses. ("We have received many anonymous, provocative messages.") All over the country people were worried about their children in summer camps, and were assured the kids were all right.

(Vienna's *Die Presse* wrote this morning:

Many people here wonder how the Czechoslovak network carries on under such difficult conditions. A well-informed Czech told us, "It's simple. One can't occupy every house in the country. The Germans learned this in Bohemia, and now the Russians are learning it." Technicians, journalists, writers, telephone operators keep the whole country informed about the dramatic events everywhere. Last night a secret television station asked its Austrian colleagues to broadcast in Czech if they should be silenced. Beginning this morning, the Austrian Radio adds a Czech-language news broadcast to its English and French news programs. . . .

The paper also reported that there was no hoarding of foodstuffs in Prague but that nervous housewives in Vienna were buying up ridiculously large quantities of sugar, flour, oil and salt.)

Radio Prague, "operating from a new location," reported on life in the capital on the third morning of the occupation. People read the free, legal newspapers and passed them on to strangers; everybody was talking to the fellow next to him; there was "a wonderful new feeling of belonging together." The Soviet soldiers sitting in their tanks read their own papers and were "plainly bewildered by the peaceful aspects of the dangerous counterrevolution." People were asked no longer to discuss politics with those "stupid, poor soldiers . . . many of them come from Asia and don't even understand Russian. . . . They are bewildered *negramotní* (illiterates)." There were sarcastic reports. Father, forgive them, for they don't know what they do. The electric streetcar wires that the tanks had ruined were being repaired, and some bus lines were operating. The National Assembly remained in session; the deputies had slept there, each getting only one blanket. The reporter said, "This morning I am proud of my fellow *Pražané* (citizens of Prague)."

It was announced that two hundred members of the KGB had been flown in from Russia in a special Tupolev. "They didn't bring along their own lists of people to be arrested but they'll probably start with the names of the people who signed 'Two Thousand Words.' Friends, be careful." Traitors were warned to think of the future. "Don't do anything now of which you may be ashamed in the future. Our people will never forget. They don't want new concentration camps."

At 9:30 A.M., President Svoboda's speech (probably earlier recorded) was broadcast. He had asked for a meeting in Moscow "to carry on negotiations for an honorable solution," and he hoped to be back that night. Peking called the invasion "a barbaric action" but did not support Czechoslovakia. Professor František Šorm, member of the Czechoslovak and the Soviet Academy of Sciences, said there was not a single collaborator among Czechoslovakia's scientists. "I never thought the Soviets would attack our country." A voice interrupted, asking everybody to watch out for automobiles with the license plates AE 4001, ABA 7119, AL 4816, and others. "These cars carry people trying to arrest our citizens. They must be stopped." (Minutes later, youngsters painted the numbers on house walls all over Prague.) Brno reported of a meeting of local Party officials with General Ivanov, who complained about "provocations of the secret radio stations which don't tell the truth." The announcer chuckled and said, "He's mad because we call the Soviets occupiers and he thinks they came to liberate us. 'General,' we asked, 'liberate from whom? From ourselves, maybe?' He didn't think that was funny and threatened drastic measures. On that cheerful note the meeting ended."

A voice from Prague warned the citizens to be careful about making accusations. "Yesterday, a certain Rychl was called a collaborator, and now a well-known friend came forward and said it was a mistake, Rychl was an honorable man. [The mistake was later explained: the collaborator's name was Richel.] We must not commit character assassination, friends, even under such difficult conditions." České Budějorice was on the air with the report of a delegate who had just returned from the secret Party Congress in Prague. "We discussed the basic things. There was complete, spontaneous unity. We didn't have much time. We had to finish before the 9 P.M. curfew. A good thing, for there was no time for useless oratory. There were Soviet tanks all around the building, but no one was afraid. It was a fine, proud meeting and gave us strength to carry on." (It was also one of the most unusual political gatherings in modern history, though the Soviets later called it an "illegal" Congress. It will remain a great demonstration of political courage. The delegates elected Dubček, in absentia, and a pro-Dubček Central Committee.) They had also formally demanded the release of all officials being detained by the invaders, the restoration of civil rights, and the immediate withdrawal of all occupation forces.

Jihlava (Iglau in Moravia, the birthplace of Gustav Mahler) was on the air now, reading an appeal to make Czechoslovakia a neutral country. Similar appeals came from other parts of the country, but some commentators explained that such demands were unrealistic and would only play into the hands of the Soviets. All newspaper dealers were warned to destroy the lists of subscribers of *Literární Listy* and *Reportér*. ("Burn them at once. The Russians want the names.")

A woman reporter had just returned from a walk through Prague. The Czechoslovak army barracks in Smíchov were surrounded by Soviet tanks. "Our soldiers looked out the windows directly into the barrels of their 'allies'' tanks. I wondered how they felt about it. It seemed straight out of Karel Čapek—or maybe Kafka." She had met a young American student. "He said, 'Prague is so beautiful, even this morning,' and then we both cried a little. . . ."

Suddenly there was the sound of voices, shouts from the rear, heavy boots, and then the radio went dead. It was 1:34 P.M. Another station cut in, saying, "We have an urgent message for Czechoslovakia Number 1, please answer, Number 1, calling Number 1." But Number 1 didn't answer. Instead there was the ominous sound of the foghorn signal. During the next three minutes—they seemed endless—there was nothing but the foghorn. Then Brno was on the air, urging people not to show their transistor radios to the Russians; they were taking them away. They'd even taken a small box from an East German tourist which they believed to be a radio. Then Brno said, "We are still waiting to hear from Prague. . . . We now connect you . . ."

Silence again . . . After a while Brno said that in Olomouc,

Moravia, all Czechoslovak Army installations had been surrounded. The garrison in Trenčín, Slovakia, was "occupied but not yet disarmed." Suddenly, Prague was back, with no explanation. Somebody read an open letter to U Thant who had cancelled arrangements to visit Prague—" for reasons known to him, we suppose, since *we* wanted very much to see him here." At 11:44 A.M., Brno reported that Soviet troops had just entered the local headquarters of the Communist Party. "Young people, get off the streets, the situation is serious. Don't give them a chance to destroy public property. In Prague, the Soviets opened fire against the monument of Saint Wenceslas and the National Museum because they thought it was Radio Prague."

At 11:48 A.M., a man said quietly, "Friends, there seems to be a little confusion in the air but relax, things could be worse. The general strike begins in eleven minutes. We will not broadcast but we are still here."

Early in the afternoon, a new station, Radio "Na Danuje" (On the Danube) joined the work with a Slovak writer's impassionate speech for unity:

> Slovaks, don't believe provocateurs that there's going to be an independent Slovakia. Personally, I would like to add that in our dark moments the Czechs and we have always been together, hand in hand, and that's the way we are now. United we shall survive. Our enemies know this well and try to divide us. . . .

There was good news at 2:10 P.M. Čestmír Cisář had escaped from police headquarters in Prague and was safe with friends who were looking after him. (Pro-Dubček secret police had managed to get Cisář away from the Soviet secret police. Several members of the Prague secret police were later arrested by the brotherly KGB) The news seemed to cheer up everybody and encourage boldness. A man said that Prague must become "a sea of resistance slogans" and that the façades "must disappear behind transparents and posters." The captains of all Czechoslovak ships were ordered to keep out of the harbors of the German Democratic Republic and were asked to go to Hamburg or a Yugoslav port instead. Railroad workers were urged to stop a Soviet train with electronic equipment that would help them locate the secret radio transmitters. (For a time, the train was "lost," on a siding in Česká Třebová, and later its electric locomotive was put out of commission when an extra-strong current was shot through the overhead wire. The train arrived at its destination several days late.)

Radio Prague warned the people that a demonstration scheduled for five o'clock in Wenceslas Square was considered a "provocation" by the Soviets. There were nearly fifty thousand people, mostly young boys and girls, standing around in the square (which is really a large boulevard). Ten minutes after the announcements posters appeared everywhere, saying "Demonstrace = Provokace." At four o'clock, Emil Zatopek, former world and Olympic champion, now a colonel in the Czechoslovak Army, toured Wenceslas Square in a loudspeaker car asking people to disperse. By five o'clock, the square was empty. There was no "provocation." Over the radio, Zatopek was warned "not to come home." He'd told the people, "We waited for the Soviets six years to liberate us, we had them with us for twenty-three years, and we won't forget them for a hundred years."

Radio Budějovice reported that a Soviet transport plane had crashed there and there were many dead and wounded. ("We lent them our own blood conserves but later the Soviet commander ordered ten Russian soldiers to donate their blood in return.") At 3:35 P.M., Prague sounded the harp melody. There was growing concern about the safety of President Svoboda who was now negotiating in Moscow. Party Secretary Cisář sent a "fighting salute" from his hideout and promised to join the new Central Committee "as soon as possible." A voice shouted, "Banská Bystrica, quickly, get off the air!" (This is a town in Slovakia.) More suspicious automobile licenses were given; this seemed to be the day of the KGB and of its collaborators.

Toward the end of the afternoon, the voices of the men and women grew tired. People seemed unable to concentrate, made mistakes, had to clear their throats often. But there was no sign of emotional fatigue, and there were more stations than before. Brno said there would be no trams and buses after eleven o'clock and urged people to stay at home. A Communist fighter since 1923, "veteran of the Spanish civil war and several wars in South America," had returned his decorations to local Party headquarters. Brno said the Soviet commander had agreed to hand over the television studio to the personnel if there should be a speech by President Svoboda. In Prague, an African student was interviewed:

> I am terribly shocked. This is no counterrevolution. The Soviets have been stupid and brutal. The nations of Africa and Asia will be deeply affected by the events in this country. My African friends and I have studied here for years, and know the people. We followed the reform, we saw new freedom, and we know that everybody is behind Dubček. The Soviet troops came here against all international rights. This intervention will have terrible consequences in Africa and Asia. We Arab and African students demand that they leave at once. . . .

There were urgent code messages, "Ludek, Mila, Vašek— everything remains," and "Jan, stay where you are." (Probably the code names of Czechoslovak Army units.) S. K. Neumann's poem "I Don't Betray" was read. Radio Budějovice announced they were on the run again, " we are trying to find a new home," and closed in style playing the Czech anthem. ČTK, the official Czechoslovak Press Agency, said they had been occupied, but were soon to operate again as "Free ČTK," and promised to continue the fight for complete freedom. Miloslav Sulek, its new director, was called a "traitor."

Shortly before 1 A.M., on August 21, Sulek had appeared at the ČTK office and demanded that an official communiqué be sent all over the world: "A Revolutionary Workers' and Peasants' Government has taken over the power in Czechoslovakia and asked the fraternal Soviet forces for aid to help the new government to suppress the counterrevolution." Sulek wanted to send out this news item personally over the telex, and was thrown out of the office by his employees "by brute force." (After Dubček's return from Moscow, Sulek was fired and replaced by Jan Suk.)

Jihlava was back on the air, this time on 188.2 meters:

"We are alive and glad that you are still alive. Can you hear us, Brno?"

"Yes, we hear you well, Jihlava."

"We had some problems here, but now all is quiet. I saw a sign today, 'We don't want the Czar but Cisář.' (Cisář is the Czech word for "emperor.") All flags are half mast in Jihlava, and the Soviets shoot into the flags. Everybody signs up for Dubček. A mother brought her two small kids and made them sign too, guiding their hands. Very few people here are known to collaborate, and we know them well and keep away from them. If they haven't learned now what freedom means they'll never learn it." (He took a deep breath.) "Let's be hopeful. At last, we are all together in this."

"Thank you, friend," said Brno. "And now we take you to Prague."

Prague expected a wave of arrests during the night and gave instructions. "When the black automobiles drive up, neighbors should give alarm. Take house numbers off. . . ." Budějovice cut in to announce they'd done it again; they'd "found a new home." A man offered "a small feature for the evening."

My wife used to say I spent too much money playing cards and drinking. Well, I told her she spent too much time nagging. Then this happened and now we sit together in our kitchen at night. I spend no more money, and she's stopped nagging for the time being. I suppose we are not the only ones that have changed. . . . Friends, it's good to know that we all belong together. As Goethe said in *Faust*, *"Blut ist ein ganz besonderer Saft."* (Blood is a very special juice).

Radio Plzeň was talking to the kids. "You've learned Russian in school but now, when the soldiers ask you anything, you don't understand them. Just shake your head and play dumb. Tomorrow is Saturday and you would like to go out bathing and picking berries in the woods. But tomorrow you will stay at home and not run around . . ." A professor of Brno's Law Faculty said they were all behind Dubček and explained, "answering many questions," that neutrality cannot be established by a unilateral declaration. It would demand the guarantees of the big powers "and you know well that such guarantees will not be given." A Czech journalist, just back from Luxembourg, was asked why the small Communist Party there supported the Soviets. He laughed. "The Party has about a dozen members who were bought by the Soviets. All intellectuals are on our side. The ruling Duchess is on our side. . . . Don't worry, friends, the entire decent world is on our side." In Prague, a woman announcer said good-bye for tonight, she was going to catch a few hours' sleep. "I hope we'll all be back tomorrow."

That Friday evening, the weekend traffic chaos was worse than ever in Vienna, owing to hundreds of small cars with "CS" license plates. There would be three or four of them, forming small convoys; the drivers didn't know their way and went slowly. The people in the cars looked bewildered. There were couples or families with children. They'd spent their vacation in Yugoslavia or, for the first time in their life, in Western Europe. There were said to be almost fifty thousand vacationers and many of them would soon pass through Vienna. This had been a great summer. Last April, the Party's new Action

Program had called for greater freedom of tavel and emigration. It promised legal provisions allowing the citizens to travel abroad more freely, to spend long periods of time abroad, and insure that they were not "unnecessarily placed in the position of unwilling emigrants." People who had escaped for political reasons before 1968 and had been called "criminals" by the Novotný regime would now be permitted to return.

Until early this year, the average citizen had great trouble in obtaining a passport. Suddenly, everybody could get one (except criminals or young men subject to military duty). There was almost no red tape. For travel to the West, a traveler needed an exit visa. It cost a little money but the great thing was that *every*body could get it. The West German Permit Office issued up to eight hundred visas a day, and the Austrian Consulate up to sixteen hundred. Many people who for years couldn't visit their friends or relatives abroad decided this was the time to go. Many went visiting the United States where there are two and a half million Czech and Slovak emigrants. Students and scientists received one-year exit permits to study abroad, and some of them received travel grants.

It was almost too good to be true. In the past, persons "who might be expected to remain abroad" or "whose staying abroad might be detrimental to the interests of the state" were refused exit visas—and nearly everybody could be denied a visa under such restrictions. Yet in the past months, exit visas had been granted to many people who had previously tried but failed to get permission to visit America or other Western countries. The Interior Ministry had also permitted wives and children of political *émigrés* to join husbands and fathers who had left the country illegally.

There were thousands of Czechoslovaks in Vienna now; in some streets one heard more Czech than German spoken. They were not refugees yet; and they were different from the Hungarians who escaped to Vienna after the Revolution, in early November 1956. The Hungarians had been in a state of shock and exhaustion, and had come with no belongings except the clothes they were wearing. In contrast, the Czechoslovak vacationers were fairly well dressed and suntanned, they had their luggage, and many had their cars. But though they looked better they were more worried than the Hungarians had been. The Hungarians had been happy to be safe; no one had thought of going back then. The Czechoslovaks faced a terrible dilemma: should they go back into an uncertain future, or go into exile? Vienna was full of rumors. One day it was said that people with valid passports were still permitted to leave Czechoslovakia, and then it was said that the issue of exit visas had been halted. Many people said they were waiting and would probably go back, unless things got "much worse." The problem was less acute for workers and employees who weren't "mixed up in politics" than for the people who had actively supported Dubček's reform—journalists, scientists, artists, physicians, writers. They loved their homeland and longed to get back; many of them had already lived through an earlier emigration. But was there any sense in going back and then being arrested by the KGB? Some tried to call up friends and relatives in Prague, but sometimes it took more than twenty hours to get through, and what could they tell you?

The people of Vienna who have not always been known for their character and efficiency, this time said little but did a lot. The Interior Ministry permitted everybody to stay in Austria, for the time being. The ex-vacationers were put up in schools, students' dormitories, the Stadthalle. The WÖK restaurant chain was offering each Czechoslovak one free meal a day. Automobilists got free gasoline tickets. Vienna's doctors, lawyers, hairdressers offered their services free of charge. Most surprisingly, even Vienna's traffic police looked the other way when a "CS" automobile was left in a no-parking zone. (Many Viennese motorists said wistfully, it would be nice to have a CS license plate, but not *really*). Many Czechoslovaks, still undecided what to do, quickly got jobs in the prosperous Austrian economy. They were said to be hard-working, taking any job they were offered, and many Austrian firms wanted more of them. The stranded Czechoslovaks set up their own efficient aid organization, distributing money, food tickets, and small German-Czech dictionaries. "We are experienced," a writer said. "This is my third emigration."

There were some Austrian dissenters—but they were a small minority—who said all this fussing about the Czechoslovaks might "provoke" the Russians, and a few Sudeten-Germans who couldn't forget that they had been expelled by the Czechoslovaks in 1945 and said it served them right. (They didn't mention what some of *them* had done to the Czechs, during the Hitler occupation; the whole history of Central Europe is one of national *ressentiments*.) Among foreign nations, the Swiss, the West Germans, the English, the Canadians and the Australians offered effective aid, visas, and often free trips paid by the country of destination for Czechoslovaks who wished to emigrate permanently. Surprisingly few people were thinking of emigrating to the United States. "Many of us have lost confidence in America," a well-known Czech writer told me, with obvious reluctance. The Swiss were issuing several hundred visas a day, and long columns form at dawn under the arcades of the Swiss Embassy in Prinz Eugen Street (almost as long as those under the arcades of the Vienna State Opera were when Karajan was to conduct.) The American Joint Distribution Committee spent, during the first weeks, an estimated sixty thousand dollars, much more than the International Red Cross, and certainly more than the Vatican which had contributed ten thousand dollars. Perhaps they cannot forget in Rome that the new refugees were the direct descendants of the Hussite "heretics."

That night, the Austrian television showed the arrival of President Svoboda in Moscow. It was well known in Vienna that the Soviet leaders had treated the Czechoslovak leaders with calculated brutality, so the welcoming ceremony, in bright sunshine, at the Vnukovo Airport, with embraces, brotherly kisses, flowers and flags had a flavor of Kafka at his strongest, most unreal. (Dear Brezhnev, the benevolent friend who told his "guests" a day later that he didn't care whether "ten thousand, or a hundred thousand or three million people in your country will die." And Svoboda, standing upright in the car on his way to Canossa, who later put down his medals of a Hero of the Soviet Union and told the Soviets that he would rather shoot himself than see his country partitioned between Czechs and Slovaks, as the Russians had demanded.

The first pictures from occupied Prague were also shown—rather murky silent films, taken by courageous cameramen at considerable personal risk. They showed burning tanks in front of the Prague Radio station, the statue of Saint Wenceslas covered with posters, and, everywhere, the bewildered yet clearly unafraid faces of young boys and girls. There was the sidewalk of Wenceslas Square, in front of the Jalta Hotel, from where I'd walked only a few days ago (yes, it seemed like ages ago) to the main railroad station that had once been called Wilson Station, in honor of President Woodrow Wilson. I had been there in the afternoon, and the sidewalks were crowded with people going home from work, doing a little shopping, tourists from West and East who had come to see the miracle of this new freedom; above all, many young people.

Prague seemed to have been taken over by the young people; it was enormously alive. In front of the Jalta Hotel, West German businessmen and Arab delegates—there were always some delegations—sipped cold drinks and looked at the pretty girls. Now two tanks stood there, surrounded by young people arguing with the Soviet soldiers, but Prague appeared just as alive as before, though in a different way. It was then that I began to hope again that the city, and the country, might stay alive and somehow save the heritage of the "Prague Spring."

Saturday, August 24, began rather ominously. All "free legitimate" stations warned the people about impending arrests. It wasn't certain whether the Russian secret police or local collaborators were responsible, or both. People were also warned to be careful when they stopped "suspicious" cars. In Prague, a man had been pulled out of a black Tatra and beaten, because they thought he was a traitor; actually he was a patriot, on an errand for the clandestine radio network. Ostrava reported that the people of Vítkovice (where the large Vítkovice Iron Works are located) had changed the name of Russian Street to Dubček Street. (Later, some towns renamed *all* streets and squares after Dubček which baffled the Russians.) A moving letter from a Czech woman to her best friend, a Russian woman, was read. The Ostrava announcer thanked for the flowers and jars of preserves which some people had brought to their secret studio. He asked the people not to print rude or obscene words on posters because "such undignified methods might be used by the Soviets against us as proof of our 'counter-revolution.'" The Czech Youth Organization appealed to young people everywhere to break off all relations with youth groups of the five Warsaw Pact countries. The miners at the Jáchymov uranium mines from where the entire production went to the Soviet Union, promised to produce "not one gram of uranium" but would say on the job in order to protect the mines against the invaders. Speaking for Prague's Theological Faculty, a man reminded his listeners of the sufferings of Christ. Food producing firms were asked to send their goods in delivery trucks showing no names, no signs, because some trucks had been robbed by hungry soldiers.

(The fraternal occupiers behaved according to national character. The Bulgarian soldiers were accused of looting shops. The Poles didn't shoot and often fraternized with the people when their officers weren't looking. The Hungarians were hated in Slovakia where people spat upon them. The East Germans, the 11th Motorized Infantry Division from Erfurt and the 7th Panzer Division from Dresden, photographed automobiles and made notes, in Gestapo fashion, for future reference.)

Prague said they were getting many calls about the Moscow

negotiations. "We are just as impatient as you," the woman announcer said, sighing. She warned people driving to Prague that the Soviets were taking away transistor radios and food. More coded messages. "Jan, the car from Karlovy Vary is on its way." "Jiří, don't give tape recordings to anyone you don't know." Mothers of young Army recruits were asked not to visit their boys. "Most barracks are surrounded but our Army officers take good care of your boys." Jihlava announced that local meat packers had large supplies ready, please send your trucks. At 10:35 A.M. a man was introduced as a close friend of Alexander Dubček:

> I've heard some people ask whether Dubček hasn't betrayed the nation. Friends, whatever the verdict of history will be about Dubček, one thing is certain: he hasn't betrayed anyone. He just isn't the type. He was never out for power—the sort of man that may become a traitor. I've been asked why he kept some people in high places that now turned against him. Because he didn't want to force the issue; he knew what he was up against. Friends, we must expect terrible months and years to come but no matter what happens don't forget Dubček who tried to give us Socialism *and* freedom, something, many people now say, that cannot be combined. They may arrest us. They may try to silence the elite of the nation. But no matter how much we lose we must never lose ourselves. We may face collective death but we must never accept national shame (*národní hanba*). . . ."

Prague interrupted with an urgent message: "Lamps for Bohemia needed. It's getting dark." In the garden of the Soviet Embassy engineers were said to set up a TV transmitter; people were asked to see what could be done about it. (The hermetically closed off Soviet Embassy became the center of power from where the occupation was directed.) On this morning, the fourth since the invasion, all Communist Party build-

64

ings in Prague had been occupied by the Soviet troops, all railroad stations and the State Bank, after the employees refused to exchange rubles into crowns, all newspapers, the Writers' Union and the Journalists' Union—"naturally," the announcer said sarcastically—all bridges, and the airports of Ruzyně and Kbely. Bread and potatoes were getting scarce. At a Communist Party office, the troops had stolen stationary and official seals and would probably forge Party identification cards. Radio amateurs were warned to operate cautiously. "We may need your help later on. *Bude tma.*" (It will be dark.) People were asked to collect and destroy Russian printed leaflets "as soon as the soldiers are out of sight." At 12:38 P.M., a Prague commentator read "Answer to an Anonymous Letter-Writer":

> You wrote that you know our names, our home addresses, everything about us. The only thing you don't know is where we are now. . . . We are not afraid of you, but we are afraid of the shame and dirt (*špina*) that people like you cause to the nation—people without a name, without a face, without identity. You want to help the enemy because you think you're helping yourself. You are tragically mistaken. You and the like of you have united our people as perhaps never before in history. Our voices in the air sing a chorale of freedom. I wonder how a man from a Czech or Slovak mother can be so despicable—but unfortunately there will always be people like you. You wrote that you hate us. Well, we don't hate you; we are sorry for you.

At this point, the announcer interrupted, "Attention, watch out for Army car, license number 28-16-80, with a Czechoslovak officer, a civilian, two Soviet soldiers. They arrest Party officials." He went on. "We have received a message from Moscow. President Svoboda and the other members of the delegation hope for an honorable solution." Another man came on to say, "Please don't be so rude to these eighteen-year-old soldiers. Most of them don't know what this is all about." A man in Ostrava said that the miners had collected thirty-three thousand signatures for the recall of the Ostrava deputy, Drahomír Kolder, whom they accused of having betrayed Dubček. The soldiers of the Opava garrison (where I had served my basic training thirty-eight years ago) had sent a strongly worded letter to the Soviet commander in Prague, to get the hell out. A man speaking from Prague said he'd seen the word "*smrt*" ("death") written on house walls under the names of collaborators, and he urged people to think twice before ruining a man who might be a decent citizen. "There are not as many traitors as some of you believe. Perhaps twenty or thirty at the Interior Ministry." It was announced that a one-page edition of *Reportér*, the Journalists' Union's magazine, was being distributed in the streets. A man reported he'd just talked to two trusted Soviet friends who were now officers in the Soviet Army. "First, I made sure that it wasn't a trap. We spent an hour together. They are heartbroken and deeply ashamed. Yes, they were crying. They said that millions of people in the Soviet Union feel as they do, and asked me to give you this message."

A man said ironically, "I just listened to the Vltava station. They call us Western imperialists. Folks, when you bring us flowers and food to our cellars, remember that we are not Czechs or Slovaks but Western imperialists. We may even be agents of the West German Bundeswehr, and we may be broadcasting from West Germany." (Two days later, TASS said that many secret stations were stationed in West Germany.) From Plzeň, a spokesman for the Škoda Works suggested making tomorrow, Sunday, a working day. "We'll work a special Dubček shift. The economy needs it. And as long as we stay in the factories, our 'dear friends' will not try to take them away from us. It'll be a general strike in reverse." Prague asked painters and artists to stay away from the Café Mánes which was surrounded. The Supraphone recording firm was distributing small records with the text of the Fourteenth Party

Congress proclamation, on one side in Czech, on the other in Russian. "Give them as souvenirs to the Soviet soldiers. We hope they'll play them when they get home." In the Žižkov district, a drunk had abused two Soviet soldiers who wanted to shoot him, and was saved when a Czech policeman arrested him. Then the drunk called the policeman a "collaborator." "Friends, such things must not happen. Imagine the consequences!"

A man just back from a trip through Bohemia said all highway signs pointed the wrong way or led into fields and stone quarries. He would have got lost if young children hadn't shown him the right way. The whole country was a labyrinth, with every road leading to Moscow. An announcer said, "If there's an accident and you call for an ambulance, wait in front of the house, or they may not find you." They were really thinking of everything. Prague asked people to destroy the directories in all public telephone booths. "A phone is no good when you don't know the number," a man said, laughing. "Besides, there are too many addresses in these directories." The technique of sabotage had reached subtle perfection. (The late Alfred Polgar, one of the best experts of Hašek's "Schweik" once wrote, "Schweik is the spirit that always says yes: a truly super-Mephistophelian trick to show that what exists is worth to perish." The Schweiks of 1968 had reverted to the super-duper-Mephistophelian trick of always saying, "I don't know.")

At 4:54 P.M., a Slovak station reported that Deputy Interior Minister Villiam Šalgovič was now officially a traitor. By order of the government, his instructions were said to be illegal. Interior Minister Pavel had personally taken over the Ministry, after an unexplained absence. Long queues were said to form in front of the electric appliance and radio stores; people needed new transistor batteries. A coded message said, "Jirko, shame on you, come home." People were warned not to let their pictures be taken by Russian soldiers; such photos might give Russian newspaper readers a false picture of fraternization. "If they insist, just turn around." (In Bratislava, ladies of the local demimonde establishment were said to react by lifting their skirts and showing the Soviet photographers their bare behind. An editor there distributed copies of a secret newspaper when he saw the former chief censor in the crowd. He put a bundle of papers in his arms, and the ex-censor had to help with the distribution. In Bratislava, they didn't lose their sense of humor. One paper, *Lud,* reprinted daily commentaries from the pre-Munich summer of 1938. In its last issue, *Kultúrny Život* printed an open letter to Stalin: ". . . Jan Hus couldn't defend his truth today. They would secretly burn him and announce over TASS that this dangerous counter-revolutionary had burned himself to discredit the working class.") After three days of pasionate and useless discussions with the Soviet soldiers, the people were now told to ignore the occupiers. "Prague," said a man, "must become an anonymous city, a silent city. Only the air will remain alive with our words. They cannot shoot words with guns."

On Saturday night, a classmate from my Ostrava *Gymnasium* days telephoned. (I shall call him M.) He had been with his wife in Yugoslavia when he heard the bad news. They had at once driven to Austria and had spent the past fifty hours trying to get in touch with their son, Pavel, a twenty-two-year-old medical student in Prague. They phoned the apartment twice and were told by a relative that Pavel was out in the streets most of the time, arguing with the Russians and demonstrating. At last, they reached Pavel at two in the morning and told him to come to Vienna at once. He didn't want to come; he said he belonged there with his friends. Only after his father told him that his mother might have a severe breakdown, Pavel had reluctantly promised to come, and he had arrived just a few hours ago.

They came to see us that night. Pavel said it hadn't been difficult at all to get out; everybody had helped him. He'd had a passport since last spring, as had almost everybody else. A friendly Czech police official gave him an exit visa and wished him luck. The Austrian Embassy had readily given him a gratis visa. In front of the legation building he met a young Frenchman who was driving to Vienna. The Frenchman had agreed to take Pavel along if he could be ready in an hour and wouldn't bring along much luggage. At the family apartment, Pavel had packed a small bag. He forgot his mother's jewelry but brought out a heavy package with underground leaflets that his friends had asked him to distribute among journalists and radio people in Vienna. I offered him a drink but he said, thanks, no alcohol. We squeezed a few organges for him. He said it was the first glass of fresh orange juice he'd had in his life.

Pavel said he might be going back. He was afraid what was going to happen now, but he hadn't been afraid in Prague. "When you are in a crowd, you are not afraid. There are so many of you. We stayed in upper Wenceslas Square and took our orders from the radio. I argued with several Soviet soldiers and officers. The crew of one tank who had been flown into Prague thought they were in the Ukraine. One soldier said, 'I've always hated those Ukrainian dogs,' and he pointed his submachine gun at the Prague students. Another group of soldiers who had been in their tank for the past two months were convinced they were in imperialist Germany. We couldn't convince them they were in Prague. They said their officer told them this was Germany. We asked them how come that all Germans spoke Czech and Russian? They said Germans were 'very clever, very dangerous.'"

In the past, people had always gone to Staroměstské Náměstí (Old Town Square) and rallied around the monument of Jan Hus at a time of national crisis. There were more historical associations in Old Town Square than elsewhere in Prague. The first Defenestration in 1419 had started the Hussite wars; in 1437, Jan Roháč of Dubná, the last great Hussite warrior, was executed in front of the Town Hall; in 1621, after the defeat at the White Mountain, twenty-seven Czech nobles and burghers were executed in front of the Town Hall; and in

1945, some Czech patriots were killed by the Nazis in this square shortly before the Russians liberated Prague. (The house where Kafka was born stands at the corner and was originally called "U Radnice," At the Town Hall.)

This time, though, no one went to Old Town Square. The Soviets, probably instructed by some local "advisers," had completely locked off the square with tanks and antiaircraft guns. In front of the Kinsky Palace (where Kafka went to the Old Town Gymnasium) there was a large banner "Russian Art of the 1920s," and in front of the banner were the tanks. Some people managed to take pictures of the newest Russian art. ("Perhaps it was just as well we couldn't demonstrate at the Jan Hus monument," said Pavel. "It's easy to get up on the monument and lie there, and that might have created trouble.")

And so the people went to Saint Wenceslas in upper Wenceslas Square that now became the symbol and center of the resistance. Even nonreligious Czechs have always felt strongly about Bohemia's patron saint. In 1929, one thousand years after "Good King Wenceslas" was murdered by his brother Boleslav I, Arne Novák wrote in *Lidové Noviny*, "Smetana, our national composer, wished that his opera *Libuše* should be performed only 'in great national moments.' In such moments we should always make a pilgrimage to Saint Wenceslas." At one time, during the Novotný regime, so many people came to pray or placed flowers at the foot of the statue that the authorities surrounded it first with a scaffold, and later with a small lawn. People were not permitted to step on the grass. The cult of Saint Wenceslas belongs to the multifaceted mysticism of Prague that has survived regimes and ideologies for the past thousand years.

And now they came again for solace and strength to Saint Wenceslas, old people, but mostly young people, in spite of the tanks that surrounded the statue. All week long the marble socle accurately reflected the people's feelings. During the first days, there were fighting slogans and fresh flowers. The slogans said that the word was stronger than the gun. A red-white-blue flag was put into the hands of the Saint. During the Moscow negotiations the slogans were replaced with pictures of Svoboda and Dubček and with banners exhorting the leaders to remain firm. And after the delegation had returned to Prague and the terrible truth became known, the pictures disappeared, and now there was the black flag of mourning in the hands of Saint Wenceslas. But underneath it still said, "We don't give up."

Sunday, August 25. The fifth day of the occupation. There were more than half a million foreign soldiers in the country but Soviet Ambassador Stepan Chervonenko had been unable to establish a collaborationist government. The legally elected bodies—the National Assembly and the government—and the highest Party groups were in permanent session. Radio Prague read an editorial:

> In the past few days you've heard many words that cannot be translated into Czech or Slovak. In this war of words we must be careful not to get trapped in the no man's land of idiocy. Our occupiers are called "brothers and helpers," our patriotic talk is "counter-revolutionary activity," our people stick together as never before are said to be divided "by imperialistic agents." Friends, you are too intelligent to be confused by this new Babylonian tower. . . . You know what happened to the original tower. This new tower will also collapse, and bury underneath their silly words. . . .

A calm voice exhorted the Czechoslovak people to remain patient; the Moscow negotiations were dragging on and fears spread that there might be "a terrible compromise." Exhausted, demoralized Soviet units had been exchanged for troops that were not yet "infected" and trigger-happy; mothers were warned to keep their children away from the soldiers. Foreign Minister Jiří Hájek's appeal to the United Nations Security

71

Council had been heard "and is already forgotten," a man commented. Incidents had been caused by "brutal, barbaric" Soviet troops. In central Bohemia, a new station introduced itself with the powerful theme song *"My jsme Boží Bojovníci,"* "We are the fighters of God" from *"Tábor,"* the fifth movement of Smetana's *My Country;* probably the station was near Tábor. In Prague, Jiří Dienstbier, the commentor, said the occupation had become a disaster for the Soviet leaders. The Polish and Hungarian troops were getting restless. There were protest demonstrations and arrests in East Germany. He had seen signs "Long Live Our Free Radio!" He added, "Maybe our own leaders in Moscow don't know how strong the country's morale is. In a referendum today, ninety-nine percent of the population would declare themselves behind Dubček." (He was exactly right. On August 31, when the worst was known, *Rudé Pravo* made a poll: ninety-nine percent were for Dubček.)

All morning, the Slovak stations assured their Czech friends of the unity of the two peoples. "Your strength is our strength," a message from the workers of Slovakia declared. People were warned to conceal mimeograph equipment, the Soviets were looking for it. In many areas rains had endangered the potato harvest, and people were asked to help out in the fields. The workers in several factories asked what to do about export deliveries to the Warsaw Pact countries. Radio Prague advised them to wait. A town in Bohemia needed chlorine to cleanse its drinking water, and the railroad workers were asked to speed up a shipment from western Bohemia. Several commentators expressed the hope that Svoboda would soon return from Moscow; people were getting very anxious; time was said to be working for the occupiers. Several labor leaders said they stood firm behind the intellectuals of the nation who had carried the banner of the reform. (No such statement had ever been heard before.) In the Prague suburb of Podolí, the Soviets had forcibly prevented the Prague police from taking wounded people to the hospital. The Soviets had failed to find collaborators among the regular Czech police; in fact, police cars had been seen distributing underground newspapers. A reporter from Prostějov, Moravia, had spoken to Hungarian soldiers "who couldn't look our people in the eye." A Prague commentator, whose mildly ironic voice had become familiar in the past days, said:

> Dear occupiers, if you listen to us, you know that we didn't desert the Socialist cause, in spite of what you did to us. Incidentally, we suggest that you rename your Vltava (Moldau) station "Volga," which will identify you. We're telling our listeners your wavelength so they can tune in and judge by themselves the level of your ridiculous, amateurish propaganda. Above all, dear occupiers, please learn to speak decent Czech and Slovak!

A woman said, "Václav, the chocolate is ready for delivery." After a pause, "Jana in Prague, the light went out." An announcer said the next speaker would address the 250,000 members of the nation's gypsy minority in their own language, Romany, and a woman made a passionate speech; all I understood were the words "Dubček" and "Svoboda." Plzeň gave the license number of an official black car on its way to Prague and asked to let the driver get through. "He is a friend. Give him all possible help." Soviet officers had asked the workers at the Škoda factories to take off the black flags but the workers "just ignored them." A voice said, "Jírko, report back, Milada." "The doctors tell me that Kolda and Volimek are dead." A girl's voice shouted, "Get ready for Number 2!" A commentator in Ostrava said:

> I woke up last night and I didn't know whether it was all true or a nightmare. Many of the Soviet soldiers don't even speak Russian. Their logic is the logic of another planet. Don't speak to them, use visual means. Show them primitively drawn posters. . . .

A new Slovak station, "Kriváň," joined the network, and said

"The envelope leaves on train 72, Pavel." Prague asked all stations whether one should play "a little music once in a while. . . . No silly tunes, of course. But we need a little free time to work on news and messages." A Czech actor read a German-language appeal,

> *Achtung!* We call Comrades Admiral Zerner, Colonel Siegfried Berthold (there followed at least a dozen other names). Here is your friend Josef Koenigsmark. I hope we are still friends and that you still believe your old friend Josef. Remember the evenings we spent together this spring and summer? You were all excited about our new Socialism, you wished me luck. . . . Now your soldiers brutally invaded our beautiful country. Our women and children are terrified. Dear friends, you were so kind to our group when we performed there not long ago—can you believe that our nation has suddenly turned against Socialism, that we are counterrevolutionaries, as you are told by your newspapers? Do you realize, that the entire population stands behind Dubček? Is it a counterrevolution when a nation suddenly discovers its true soul? If you don't believe me, friends, then we can no longer be friends. But if you do believe me, spread the word, tell the truth to everybody, help us in this terrible hour. Your troops shoot at our people while your leaders talk of peace and friendship. Come back, my dear friends, but do not bring weapons, and we shall receive you with open arms. For God's sake, stop this terrible invasion! Call your soldiers back home!

Radio Brno asked people to remove the swastika signs and pictures of gallows which were "undignified," and replace them with pictures of Dubček and Svoboda. "We don't want to see the swastika next to the Communist star. Even in this terrible hour, the star remains the symbol of Socialism. Remember, the star belongs to us too, not only to those who betrayed Socialism. The star belongs to all who fight against Brezhnev's,

74

Ulbricht's, Gomulka's new imperialism. The star remains the symbol of the working class and no one has exclusive rights to it—certainly not the troops in their tanks with the star."

Ivan Křiž, head of the Moravian Writers' Union, denied rumors that the people of Moravia wanted their own statute in the new federation:

> We, the writers of Moravia, take our place among our Czech colleagues in the National Council. Please give my message to Comrade Cisář. We Moravian writers are with you, and you can rely on us. . . . Give our greetings to our Czech friends, Goldstücker, Kohout, Vaculik, Liehm—to all of them.

Radio Brno said that General Pavlovsky was furious about signs "*Veni, Vidi, Fugi.*" Their station was in favor of sending little music, "provided it is protest music." It was announced that several young people in Brno and Gottwaldov had demonstratively joined the Communist Party, to show their solidarity. High school students were told to get ready for their entrance examinations next Monday. The daughter of the late Zdeněk Nejedlý, who had been a noted musicologist and one of the earliest Communist leaders, said, "My father was a member of the Soviet Academy of Science. He was twice awarded the Order of Lenin. And now I must protect my children against the soldiers of Brezhnev. Please go away—you've made a fateful mistake!"

At 11:16 A.M. Station Number 1 warned all doctors helping wounded people to be careful; there was again shooting in Prague. The Czech Women's Association sent a message to the wives of Dubček, Černik, Kriegel. "We Czech women suffer with you. You are not alone. After all, there are seven million of us." (Mrs. Dubček, who had been in Yugoslavia with two of her three sons when Czechoslovakia was invaded, had returned to her home in Bratislava; the third son has also gone back. The boys told an interviewer they were all right, the neighbors helped them. "If we are taken away, people will know about it.") At 12:25, a telegram from General Svoboda to the chief of staff of the Czechoslovak Army was read: ALL IS WELL, KEEP CALM, WE HOPE TO BE HOME SOON AGAIN. In Hungary, many Czechoslovak tourists were not permitted to cross the Czechoslovak border and would have to return by way of Austria. The writers of Hungary and Poland were asked, "Don't write lies about us! Have confidence in us and investigate before jumping to wrong conclusions!"

A Prague commentator said:

> In Munich, in 1938, our Allies betrayed us but they didn't attack us. Friends, today's betrayal is worse than Munich. But we've won earlier battles with the silent weapons of moral strength. None among us has capitulated. The world listens to our free, legitimate radio stations. Our newspapers get printed. Parliament remains in session. . . . Let us try to remain patient no matter what Vltava says. They try to create the climate of panic. They would provoke incidents so their troops could turn Prague into a second Budapest. Keep away from them! Not a glass of water even! When these soldiers return home, they will talk to their comrades; they will never be the same. The Soviet generals have shown the world the barbaric side of Czarist Russia. Don't ask for neutrality, friends; this would be a dangerous illusion. Our true weapons are silence and the truth!

At 12:20 a Slovak station said that a Soviet unit had opened fire on a Bulgarian unit whom they considered "counterrevolutionaries." A man from Čadča, Slovakia, said he was almost ashamed to report that theirs was a happy district, there was only one armored vehicle in town, everybody was praying for the rest of the country on this lovely Sunday morning. The station "Kriváň" was called but didn't answer. The city authorities in Mariánské Lázně (Marienbad) had turned down an invitation to meet with the local Soviet commander, saying "We can take care of our affairs." Several trucks loaded with vegetables and potatoes were on their way to Prague but no one knew when they would arrive, "because they cannot take the shortest route." At 14:05 P.M., Ostrava reported that this was the first Sunday in people's memories when everybody was working. A Prague commentator said:

> . . . The staging is bad, and the producers in Moscow are getting angry. Goodness, they treat us as though we were Indians in a reservation in America. The little men in the Kremlin didn't learn the lessons of history. The successful invaders—Caesar, Alexander, Napoleon, Hitler—never made such a mistake. Even our secret police refuses to collaborate. After six days their aggression has no veneer of legality. It isn't very pleasant to have half a million soldiers here and not to know what to do with them. Even the morons know that they are not in West Germany. . . . The Kremlin has done it at last: they created their own Vietnam in Czechoslovakia—

A woman's voice cut in, "Kriváň, get out, they're coming after you!"

> . . . We must realize that if our leaders in Moscow don't accept their terms, we will remain occupied, maybe for a long time. Later, the Soviets may get more desperate and attack Romania or Yugoslavia. We watch the sorry spectacle of the world's two biggest powers caught in their own traps. . . . Let's be realistic, friends. We cannot get out of the Warsaw Pact. I don't ask you to accept capitulation but I ask for your patience until our leaders return and tell us what happened. Let's be *realistic* (his voice underscored the word) and demonstrate to the whole world that our conscience is clear. . . .

Apprehension was spreading on Sunday afternoon; people were afraid of what the next hours would bring. Čierná and

Tisou sent greetings to everybody. The Košice hospital needed blood donations. Ostrava said it was a "dead city," but the factories were alive, going full blast. (*Mrtvé město, živé závody.*) Instructions told the television owners how to turn their antennas in a special way to receive the new program. A. C. Milano, a famous soccer club, had called off its match in Bulgaria. A man said, "When you notice something strange happening nearby, call the neighbors, turn on all lights, call the police, *do something.*" A garrison town in Bohemia reported that many girl friends of Czechoslovak soldiers were waiting in front of the barracks. "Don't be disappointed, girls. The boys are restricted this weekend. They didn't forget their dates with you. . . . We all wish these restrictions would end. Go home and be good." The free radio was certainly in touch with the people.

East German tourists in Prague were told, in German, they need not worry about hostile reactions from the populace. "Our people know the difference between you and those who gave the shameful orders." (Two East German students were seen in Wenceslas Square carrying placards, WE ARE ASHAMED OF BEING EAST GERMANS.)

Late on Sunday afternoon, the tree-shaded street below my apartment windows in Vienna was quiet and peaceful. The sun had all but gone down, and the line of the distant hills in the east, toward Czechoslovakia, stood out clearly against the darkening sky. A few strollers were on their way home from Türkenschanzpark, named after the fortifications that the Viennese put up in 1683, prior to the Second Turkish siege. Gambling on the dissension of the German princes and the confusing jealousies among Austria's allies, the Turks had sent an army of 230,000 men against Vienna. The Vienna garrison of sixteen thousand men withstood the siege and was at last relieved on September 12, when the Turks were beaten back. Western civilization was saved.

At the street corner, a car was parked and a group of people was listening to a transistor radio. I heard Czech words. The Viennese walked politely past the small car that had a Prague license number. . . . Late that evening, Radio Warsaw reported on a TASS correspondent's visit to an "underground" radio station in Czechoslovakia which had been discovered by what were called the "allied" troops. The station had been hidden in a subterranean stronghold on a wooded hill, using "much modern equipment from abroad." (About that time the "free, legitimate" radio reported that the Žilina station, in Slovakia, had been occupied by the Soviets.) In Plzeň the Soviets destroyed one of the country's most modern television stations that night.

A Czech radio technician later told me in Vienna that many small stations had been set up during the Novotný regime, at the urging of Soviet experts who said that such a network might be needed one day to swiftly inform the population against an invasion from the West. After the collapse of the Novotný regime, the radio people had quietly changed the structure and direction of the network against a possible invasion from the East. ("The thought never disappeared from the back of our minds though we avoided talking about it," the technician says.) Moscow claimed that the equipment had been produced in West Germany and was smuggled in by way of Austria. The Free Prague Radio stated that "the microphones were made in Austria, some of the machines in Germany, and the tapes in Switzerland." At certain times the free broadcasts were channeled into local telephone circuits and people could hear them by dialing certain numbers. Radio Moscow reported that one underground station had been set up in the garden of a certain Western embassy in Prague. (Most embassies have gardens.) The technician laughed. "We didn't need the protection of an exterritorial garden," he said. "In a few days, our network was operating beautifully everywhere."

On Sunday night, a special-delivery letter arrived from Paris.

My friend J., the amateur-historian, had arrived there two days before the invasion. His children were in Prague and he thought he would have to return, even if this would mean jail, "or worse." He was depressed. "It is no consolation that not only we were stupid—though I never excluded the possibility from my thoughts—but most of the world too. . . . The situation will be remarkable from a historical viewpoint but difficult for us as individuals. Eventually things may settle one way or the other, and some people will again say, "We've exchanged a great time for a smaller one! . . . Jarmila, poor girl, is there. She's been through one concentration camp, and now another may await her. . . ."

The early news broadcast of Radio Vienna, on Monday, August 26, featured a correspondent's report from Prague that had been received at two in the morning. He said he was speaking from a house near the main railroad station. There was so much shooting that sometimes his voice couldn't be heard, and it was remarkable that he was still able to telephone. All lights had gone out, and everybody was very nervous. He'd heard a story of a collaborator being lynched but couldn't confirm it. There was more shooting, and the Austrian announcer's voice said that this was the end of the report.

A Slovak station said a Russian gasoline tank train was on its way to Prague, and asked the population to stop the train. Prague cut in and a man said, "Friends, you just heard the news about the tank train. Don't answer that summons. At this time when our delegation in Moscow is fighting for our national existence, such an action would only give the Soviets a good argument. Counterrevolution means something active; so far our resistance has been passive. There's no need for the population-at-large to interfere with the train. Our able railroad workers will take care of this matter." The Slovak station came back on the air, and said they agreed with the friends in Prague, they had been hasty. Another man said, if the worst happened, many Slovaks would again become Partisans in the woods, as they had been twenty-three years ago against the Germans. Many former Partisans are now with the police and the army.

Industrial enterprises were asking the radio stations to transmit urgent messages. Badly needed raw materials hadn't arrived and production might soon be halted. (This did not seem the time to discuss economic problems but many people must have wondered what was going to happen to the country's economy that depended to a large extent on Soviet raw materials.) The Louny district in Northern Bohemia urgently needed two thousand people to help harvest the hops. A man in Prague said, "The Russian soldiers seem to be getting afraid of our people who in turn are afraid of the future. The situation is absurd." Members of the Catholic dioceses were asked to have all church bells in the country ring at precisely nine o'clock that morning for fifteen minutes. Factory sirens and automobile horns would join in, for "a demonstration of national unity that would be heard in the smallest, most remote hamlet."

Radio Prague transmitted what a man called "the sounds of freedom," and in between there were people's voices. A woman said, "Do you think that the Good Lord is listening too?" and another woman answered, "It would be more important if the whole world could hear us." More messages were read asking for the early return of President Svoboda. Two Swiss boys in a small car were on their way to Prague and people were asked to help them. Radio Ostrava interviewed a Russian woman who was overcome with emotion, almost unable to speak. She said she was deeply ashamed and implored the soldiers to go home, and then she broke down and wept. After a few seconds, a man said quietly, "Dear friends, I believe no comment is needed."

A message said, "Milena stays where she is, please don't be angry, Jan." A reporter told of the nine o'clock demonstration in the streets of Prague. "A group of Soviet soldiers asked me what the noise meant. I said it was a referendum for Dubček, but they didn't understand. I explained that the whole country wanted to show that they stood behind their leaders. They asked me who gave the order. I said it was a spontaneous thing. It was hopeless. They didn't understand, and I walked away."

Radio Bratislava warned television stations all over the world not to accept an old film showing a friendly scene between Svoboda and Brezhnev that had been made in Bratislava after the Declaration. "They now say it was shot in Moscow after Svoboda's arrival. This is a lie." Prague explained that many stations had to change their frequency at short notice because things were getting tough. A new station had joined the network, broadcasting to the Hungarian minority. The "free legitimate" network was now broadcasting in Czech, Slovak, Polish, Russian, Ruthenian, Hungarian, the gypsy language, English, French and German. Prague said that leaflets had appeared asking the population to give the soldiers poisoned food and beverages, and warned of "such a stupid provocation." Ostrava interrupted: "Motorists, stay away from the road to Svinov! Soviet soldiers pull down all Dubček posters and shoot at every vehicle." A hospital in Olomouc reported that since the invasion twenty-two children had been born there, thirteen boys and nine girls. A man who seemed almost in a state of shock, told his audience how the Soviets had entered the television studio he was working in the night before. "They destroyed all equipment and shot all over the place, and they were *laughing!*" he said. "They thought it was great fun." Liberec (Reichenberg in the former Sudetenland) reported it had become a maze where strangers got lost; well-made new street signs, most of them with the name of Dubček, had been put up during the night.

A Prague commentator said the Soviets had made an interesting discovery: once again it was all the fault of the Jews. The counterrevolution was directed by "Zionists." "First, they discovered a cache of American arms near our National Theatre. Now they found two million Zionists among us.

Friends, our dear occupiers underestimate our memories. Of the three hundred and fifty thousand Jews who once lived here, less than fifteen thousand are with us . . . And they belong here." He might have added that Czech intellectuals had been unanimous in condemning the wave of anti-Semitism in Poland. *Práce,* the trade-union paper, took a firm stand on the issue by first publishing an anonymous anti-Semitic letter that blamed Jews for high prices, poor streets, dilapidated houses and queues in shops, and later published many other signed letters that condemned the anonymous letter writer. One quoted the Czech actor Jan Werich who said, "Anyone making a difference between a Jew and a non-Jew, a Christian and a non-Christian, a Communist and a non-Communist is in my eyes an idiot." *Student* had published an appeal of the Academic Council of Students of the Philospohical Faculty of Prague's Charles University to sign petitions calling for a resumption of diplomatic relations with Israel which the Novotný regime broke off during the war against the Arabs. There are fifteen hundred Czechoslovak Jews in Vienna, as I write this. They say that at no time during the week of resistance had there been any sign of anti-Semitism in the country.

A Prague journalist spoke about the disappointing meeting of the Security Council of the United Nations that had produced a resolution condemning the Soviet Union and calling for a withdrawal of all occupying troops, only to have it vetoed by the Soviet Union:

> We expected a miracle . . . but I believe the only miracle is happening here. The occupiers have done all they could to incite hatred but our people remain composed. We remain a Socialist country. We don't hate the people of Russia, East Germany, Hungary, Poland, Bulgaria. We treat their soldiers as though they were made of thin air. . . . We know that General Svoboda had a terrible time in Moscow but he is an old front soldier and we trust him. . . . Let me

finish with something I just overheard in Wenceslas Square. A sixteen-year-old boy said to a girl, "There were not only two. The third man was also dead."

Ostrava was on the air again, "after a forced interruption." The job was getting very difficult but they were all in a good mood. There were no collaborators in their city. Yesterday evening, there was an explosive situation in Rynek (the Old Town Square). Thousands of angry workers had gathered there and then the tanks came and began shooting over the heads of the people. "We quickly told people to beat it, and they dispersed, and then we played the anthems, and after a while the tanks left, and chaos was prevented."

(I could almost see the Rynek—our house in Těšínská Street had been just a block away. The baroque pestilence column in the middle, to remind people of the "black death" in the sixteenth and seventeenth centuries, when the plague had killed off half the population; the Old City Hall in the rear; my mother's beautiful stationery store to the right of it; and, twice a week, on market days, the open-air stands with flowers, vegetables, fruit.)

Plzeň reported that the technical department at the Interior Ministry in Prague had just been occupied and hoped there would be no collaborators among the officials. (There were none, it was later confirmed.) The families of two "traitors," Kolder and Indra, had sought refuge at the Soviet Embassy, "no comment needed." A big sign on the house where Kolder's family had lived said, "Traitor Kolder lives on the fifth floor." A Slovak writer said there was no more difference between Czechs and Slovaks—only between decent and bad people, patriots and traitors. A woman announcer in Prague said, the No. 10 streetcar was again running normally but did not stop in front of the Prague Radio building that was surrounded by Soviet tanks since the first hours of the invasion. She went on, "Last night Soviet soldiers shot into a group of young people. Several were killed and others were wounded. Our ambulances were not permitted to take them away. One of the ambulances was shot at. Citizens, you will remember this night until you die!" Her voice broke. Radio Plzeň announced that two streets had been renamed after T. G. Masaryk, and read an ad from the latest issue of a local underground newspaper. "To all occupiers: will trade three large pitchers of milk for a thimble of common sense."

Czechoslovakia's writers and political journalists made much common sense during this week of unreality. They were the unsung heroes of the early revolution, and later became, together with the radio and television workers, the leaders of the resistance. The public revolt of the members of the Writers' Union, in June 1967, was the beginning of the end of the Novotný regime. Some say that the *very* beginning was the meeting of a hundred Marxist philosophers, literary critics and writers, in the spring of 1963, at Castle Liblice, near Prague. Its official purpose was the "ideological clarification" [read: rehabilitation] of Franz Kafka who had been an unperson during the Stalinist regimes of Gottwald, Zápotocký, and Novotný. The meeting climaxed in the moving appeal of Ernst Fischer, the prominent Austrian Communist philosopher who exclaimed, "Get Kafka's work back from involuntary exile! Let's give him a permanent visa!" It was at this meeting that the compatibility of Socialism and freedom was for the first time discussed.

The writers and political journalists supported Dubček all the way, objectively and courageously, under very difficult conditions. They kept a delicate balance between not saying openly certain things that might be too dangerous yet keeping the population completely informed. After the Bratislava Declaration, Party Ideologist Cisář had asked for "a quiet, realistic, serious tone" in the coverage "of all events concerning the other Socialist countries." The leading editors of the mass media received a thirty-five-page list comprising "state, economic and official secrets" from the Interior Ministry. The journalists said they would not start any attacks but would not tolerate being attacked by the "fraternal" countries. They served notice that the uneasy truce would not refer to "internal" matters, knowing of course that nearly every internal matter might be interpreted by *Pravda* as a violation of the Bratislava Declaration.

"We cannot afford to lose our readers' confidence," an editor had told me in Prague. "Whenever we omit something important there start rumors that censorship has been *de facto* re-established." Many responsible journalists worried about inexperienced, younger colleagues who wrote stories that were promptly picked up by the Moscow papers. Just during the week preceding the Čierná conference, *Student* published a disastrously timed article about Radio Free Europe and the Czechoslovak émigrés in Munich. "Pravda" means "truth," but Moscow's *Pravda* has long made a parody of its name. Last July, it published a letter allegedly written by "a big group of workers" at the Praga automobile factory, "dissociating themselves from demands for the Soviet troops to leave Czechoslovakia." It was signed by sixty workers and thirty-nine workers' wives. *Pravda* didn't bother to inform its readers that the factory had over 4500 employees, most of them then on vacation, and that the letter was not discussed among the work force before it was sent to the Soviet Embassy in Prague. The bewildering gyrations of the brotherly Soviet newspapers, turning on and off vicious propaganda at a moment's notice, revealed an almost schizophrenic state of mind. Two days after Dubček had been called "a devil, a traitor, a counterrevolutionary," he was again mentioned as the Party's First Secretary.

Throughout the "Prague Spring," the leading Czechoslovak publications were alive with ideas and full of information. The writing and reporting in *Literární Listy*, bought every week by 300,000 intelligent, critical readers, was as good as the best in New York, London, Paris. Yet for a whole generation Czechoslovakia had not been a paradise for good journalism which was often a submissive game, and at best a tongue-in-cheek technique under the Nazis and later under the Stalinists. Yet now there suddenly emerged a group of political writers, many of them about forty years of age, who became eloquent spokesmen for freedom that they hadn't known—or only theoretically—during their adult lives. Some, in fact, had once been Stalinists. (Kohout, the author of the stirring appeal, wrote political poetry in the early 1950s which he later didn't care to remember; and he was not the only one.) Many atoned for their past; one called himself "an accomplished hangover expert." All of them revived the humanist traditions of Jan Amos Comenius, the seventeenth-century philosopher, and of František Palacký, the Moravian protestant, who had the courage to write, "With all my holy love for my nation I consider the interests of humanity and science more important than nationality."

Political journalism remained alive during the nineteenth-century period of national revival, under the Habsburgs. One of the best writers, Karel Havliček-Borovský, who trained a generation of gifted pupils, died in 1856. Tomáš Masaryk wrote political journalism in his young years; so did Jaroslav Hašek, and many others. Czech writers have always practised political journalism as an avocation, somewhat as French writers write on gastronomy and the British on travel. During Masaryk's First Republic, the best journalists gathered around *Lidové Noviny,* among them the brothers Josef and Karel Čapek. Plans had been made to publish again *Lidové Noviny* in October, under the sponsorship of *Literární Listy,* and the editorial offices were to be in a gloomy building in Benedikt Street that had just been vacated by the censorship office. Interior Minister Josef Pavel had released the building, and the editors had sent him a telegram with the old Czech blessing, *"Zaplať Pan Bůh!"* (May God repay you for this).

During the "Prague Spring," the journalists had to cope with the subtleties of ideological nomenclature and political semantics. "There is no longer plain Socialism," a writer said to me in Prague. "There is Mao's doctrine, the Soviet doctrine which, they claim, is Leninism; Castroism, Titoism. There is the Socialism of the Italian and French Communists, quite different from Ulbricht's and Gomulka's, and now there is our Socialism. And everybody claims he's got the right one. Yuri Zhukov writes in *Pravda* that we've betrayed Leninism. And the Albanian radio in Tirana claimed that the Soviet Union was plotting a conspiracy with the United States and West Germany which had been prematurely revealed by Dubček. Pure Socialist science-fiction."

The semantic problem began with the confusing spectrum of Czechoslovakia's Communist Party. At one end were the expendable conservatives, such as Novotný, who no longer had the support of Moscow. Next were the conservatives for whom Moscow indicated support, the ones claiming that Dubček's reform "might hurt Socialism." There was also a bloc of neoconservatives who favored economic reform but not political democratization—a position that the reformers dismissed as impossible. Toward the other end of the spectrum there were the cautious progressives, and, beyond them, the all-out reformers—the writers, intellectuals, students, and the economists around Professor Ota Šik. In the middle were the centrists who, in Dubček's words, "cannot permit a disintegration of the existing structure of political power until it can gradually be replaced by a new one." Many people believed that Dubček was always a middle-of-the-road Communist— in Prague, not in Moscow.

"Much was said and written about brother parties, brotherly unity, brotherly cooperation," Jaroslav Putik wrote during the week of Čierná. "The dictionary defines 'brotherly' as 'between brothers and closest relatives; friendly, kind, helpful.' But we were certainly not treated like brothers. Ironically, the word brother took on the opposite meaning: Cain was a brother too. Before we use the word 'brother' ever again, it will have to be disinfected. We'll have to try to make the words once again mean just what they mean." In Prague it was said, prior to the invasion, the difference between brothers and friends is that you can choose your friends but not your brothers.

Throughout the much-too-short "Prague Spring," *Literární Listy* was the birthplace of liberal thought and focus of humanist tradition: the Bible of the reformers. On August 31, Moscow's *Pravda* called the paper "a wasps' nest of counterrevolution that must be extinguished," unintentionally paying great homage to a very great newspaper. Three days earlier, *Literární Listy* published its last edition for some time to come. It had only four pages, owing to the circumstances. One cartoon showed a Soviet tank and the caption, "Proletarians of all countries unite—or we shoot." Jan Procházka, a courageous Communist, who had once been expelled from the Central Committee, by order of Novotný, wrote:

> . . . With tanks one cannot suppress people's longing for freedom. You cannot shoot at thoughts: there are not enough prisons in our country for all who wanted to carry the flag of freedom. . . . The Soviet Union has returned to the tried traditions of Cossack diplomacy. I expect that ultimately all will have to defend themselves who mortally wounded the prestige of the Soviet Union and Socialism: Brezhnev, Podgorny, Kosygin, Ulbricht, Gomulka, Kadar and Zhivkov. These are the names of the crusaders of our century.

But the most significant contribution to the special edition was written by Jan Drda, the President of the Writers' Union during the Stalinist era, and one of the most prominent Stalinist writers in Czechoslovakia, who had to retire after the beginning of the intellectual revolution. Drda wrote:

> I've been as in a nightmare since news reached me that Soviet tanks crossed our borders with the infamous purpose of occupying the country. It was incon-

ceivable; up to the very last day I told my children that this could not happen. This was the most terrible shock of my whole life, the destruction of all my beliefs, when I saw our Soviet friends in front of our house. This is a horrifying awakening, my heart is broken, my world is a shambles. . . . I cannot go on writing. I am trembling with pain, sorrow and shame. But this is the truth and I am willing to die for it. Death nearly missed me on May 6, 1945, when I stood in front of an S.S. squad of executioners. Go home, do realize your fearful mistake! I am a Czech, a Communist, a writer. I had to confess this to redeem my soul.

Jan Drda's confession explains why the Soviets found no prominent collaborators even among their former Stalinist friends.

That night I met Mrs. O. in the house of a friend. She'd just arrived in Vienna, and she looked remarkably cheerful and energetic after working six days and nights for the "free, legitimate" television network in occupied Czechoslovakia. (Incidentally, she permitted me to use her full name but she might go back soon, and I decided against it.) She said I shouldn't be deceived by her appearance; she was still "in a protracted state of euphoria." She said, "I expect it won't last after I've been here a few days." It didn't.

They woke her at one-thirty in the morning on Wednesday, August 21. "I'd been working for twelve years for our radio and then for television, and I knew this was serious. Ten minutes later, they called me again from the radio and gave me the news. I called some other people who worked with me. All of us had been in close touch with top Party and government leaders, but no one had expected this. Everybody was worried, of course. Some said the reform was going too fast. But now they had come, and they were approaching from five directions."

At three in the morning, Mrs. O. had arrived at the entrance

90

to the Radio Prague station, always a neural center. People were already milling around. Many were crying. Some were furious and said they'd been betrayed by their own leaders. She went around with a cameraman. He filmed the crowd and she interviewed people with a small tape recorder. At five they drove up to Hradčany Castle and continued their work there until six tanks approached. Five passed by, but the soldiers in the last tank saw them and stopped. One man jumped out, pointed a machine gun at them, tore the film out of the camera and took her tape recorder away.

"The worst part of it was that he spoke German," she told me. "An East German in front of our Hradčany. . . . When we got back into town, the building of Radio Prague was already occupied. We met in one of our studios and set up a sort of network. Everything was improvised. We worked in military barracks and in militia barracks. The militia had much better equipment than we had. Theirs was from the West. Everybody helped us. The Russians occupied three TV studios in Prague but they didn't find fifty other places where we had various equipment. In the beginning we had no sound track, of course, only pictures. For a while we worked from a research institute, and there we had only sound, no pictures. The idea was to be on the air all the time, to give people courage. We couldn't compete with radio so far as news was concerned. Instead we recorded interviews with political leaders and commentators."

The Soviets destroyed the main TV transmitter in Prague but the imaginative Czech technicians discovered an unfinished hotel building on a hill in the suburbs from where they arranged a connection to a transmitter in Ústí nad Labem. "There were no hills between our location and the transmitter. And we were well protected by the masons and construction workers. The first night we slept a little, wrapped in newspapers, but later we had sleeping bags. We got hot food from a nearby military (Czechoslovak Army) hospital. We had a telephone. We would use only first names when we talked to other stations. Transportation was no problem. The soldiers gave us jeeps and staff cars, and we could stop any cab driver. When we told him we were working for our television, they would take us anywhere, free. A man who ran a gasoline station supplied us, also free. At the kitchen of the military hospital they wouldn't tell the people where they sent food in thermos containers but then they were asked whether it was for the Russians, and they told the truth. Afterward, all the people in the suburb wanted to send us food. A woman brought us the keys of her apartment, and said we could sleep there. After three days everybody within a ten-kilometer radius knew where we were, but no one gave us away. We went all over Prague, fetching Party people for interviews, supplying them with food and newspapers. Once the Soviets had cut off the street, but the construction workers gave us their overalls, and we walked out between the Soviet soldiers. People in the street recognized us though we wore dark glasses, and they shook hands with and thanked us, and blessed us."

Mrs. O. was never aware of any danger. She would drive into town with an envelope, and somewhere an unknown man would wait for her, with another envelope. They would exchange a slogan, and the envelopes. She went with a TV team into the Českomoravská-Kolben-Daněk factory where the secret Fourteenth Party Congress was held. "It was in a large hall in the oldest part of the factory, where you were lost in a maze of corridors and stairways without a guide. Even if the Soviets had come into the factory, they would never have found the hall. Many prominent Party people slept there while the KGB was looking for them in their homes. After the Russians set up their Vltava television station, we noticed that they had three announcers whose faces were never shown. Their voices would be heard and meanwhile they would show lovely pictures of Hradčany and Charles Bridge. We finally tracked down the voice of one announcer, Jiří Lukáš, who had been a faithful Novotný man.

Then *we* showed a photograph of Lukáš, and told the people to take care of this collaborator. . . . After five days we had four different television programs going at the same time. In normal times, there was only one program; it had been planned to have a second one in 1972. And now, with all the tanks and guns and soldiers around us, we had four programs." She shook her head as though she couldn't believe it. "It's strange," she said. "Never in my whole life have I experienced such a complete sense of freedom as I did during these days and nights of the occupation."

I got more radio stations during the night than in daytime but it was harder to keep them apart. That night, as I turned the knob, I suddenly heard two different voices. Both spoke Czech but the words had a different meaning. One station was easy to recognize—one of the "free, legitimate" stations. Overlapping was another voice. A man said that the counterrevolutionaries had failed and that the allied troops had been able to restore "peace and order" in Prague. Just then the free station reported that heavy shooting was heard from the park in front of the main railroad station and that the tracer bullets lit up the dark sky. "No one knows why the Soviets are shooting. Maybe they are afraid." Meanwhile, the man on the other station read a report from *Pravda,* something about brave people in Czechoslovakia, who were "unafraid to welcome the armies of peace." At that point, I remember, I turned off the radio, and went to bed.

At six in the morning, on Tuesday, August 27, Radio Vienna reported that President Svoboda "and all other members of the Czechoslovak delegation" had returned to Prague before dawn. Since 5:25, the Presidential flag had been flying again over Hradčany Castle. A little later, the news was confirmed by the "free, legitimate" stations. The workers of the Vítkovice Iron Works sent their greetings to the President and asked him "to tell the people as soon as possible that the reforms will not be sacrificed." Everybody was clearly apprehensive about what the next hours would bring. An issue of *Rudé Pravo*, that had been secretly printed during the night, published on its front page a quotation from Karl Marx: "Only that nation is free which does not deprive another nation of its liberty." In Bucharest, the Politiburo of the Romanian Communist Party was meeting to discuss the Soviet threat. (Romania's Warsaw Pact allies have long-standing territorial demands: Hungary wants Transylvania and Bulgaria wants Northern Dobrudja from the Romanians.)

A sober mood was spreading. A man from Radio Prague, apparently sensing the mood of the people, suggested once more a powerful demonstration at nine o'clock—church bells, factory sirens, automobile horns, "even alarm clocks"—"to greet the return of our delegation." The Soviets had fired shots against a children's hospital. A coded message, "The water is rising" was repeated several times. An actor read the scene from Karel Čapek's play, *R.U.R.*, in which the robots are about to take over the world and a man, reassuring himself that there are still other human beings alive in the electrical plant, says, "Ah, they're there, and they are working." The actor paused and interpolated, "Remember nine o'clock, so it will be said, 'They're there, We can still hear them.'"

An Austrian reporter later telephoned from Prague to Radio Vienna:

> At nine o'clock, there was an incredible demonstration. I was in a side street of Wenceslaus Square. Suddenly I heard the church bells and factory sirens, automobilists and bus drivers sounded their horns, an old woman beat an iron stick against an empty garbage can, a cook and his helpers came running out, beating spoons and ladles against pots, from the windows people held out ringing alarm clocks, and those who had nothing in their hands just yelled and shouted. It was a wonderful madhouse of a wonderful free spirit, and it brought tears to my eyes. . . .

After fifteen minutes, Radio Prague had urgent messages: a chemical factory was asked to send two cisterns of glycerin, there were enough potatoes in the shops of Prague, Ústí (Aussig) in Northern Bohemia offered waterproof dyes, "so that new signs can be painted that won't be washed down by the rain." Radio Plzeň, "always happy to give you some good news," broadcast a reporter's interview with Soviet soldiers:

> I asked them whether they believed there was a counter-revolution in our country, and they said, "Brezhnev said so, and it must be true." I asked, "Suppose Brezhnev tells you something contrary next week, and they said, "Then *that* will be true." Then I got exasperated and asked, "Does that mean that whatever Brezhnev says is true?" and they all gravely nodded and said, "*da, da.*" [Yes, yes.] I thought I'd heard this before—many years ago, when Goebbels was still around. Then they said now they would ask *me* something: exactly *where* in West Germany were all our secret radio stations?

Another man said, "Friends, what is the Soviet soldiers' most important piece of military equipment? Answer: eye shades and ear pads." He also told people to buy DDT "which is good against *šváby* and *rusy.*" ("Swabians" and "Russians" are argot expressions describing particularly obnoxious species of vermin and beetles.) They were trying to cheer up the people. Radio Prague suddenly interrupted, "Don't mill around in front of the *Práce* [trade-union paper] building—a tank is hidden in the doorway."

It was reported that Czechoslovak troops were again guarding Hradčany Castle. The Soviet troops had moved away. "Answering many anxious questions, we want to assure everybody that all our leaders, including Alexander Dubček, are now meeting at the Castle." (People were not told that when Dubček arrived in his car at a back entrance and stepped out, he collapsed in a faint and had to be carried in. Radio

95

Vienna later broadcast a medical bulletin that Dubček suffered from "complete nervous exhaustion." Belgrade reported he had been taken to a hospital that was "guarded by the Soviets." There were more rumors than news.)

Prague was said to be "more normal" this morning. The streetcars were running, the Soviet tanks had left the Vltava bridges and were now in the suburbs. From Pankrác (the name of a suburb synonymous with Prague's largest prison) a long tank column was moving toward Tábor, and "possibly toward the Austrian border."

Suddenly there were excited voices. A woman was heard crying, and she said, "Friends, we have Comrade Smrkovský here. . . ." Then there was silence, and Smrkovský said, very softly, "*Těžko se mně mluví . . .*" (It's hard for me to speak). His flat, broken voice heavy with exhaustion and emotion, was the most shocking thing I had heard so far. Smrkovský, the most cheerful and loud-voiced among the reform leaders, always glad to address a crowd, was now barely audible, unable to keep his voice under control, as he said that he was "bowing deeply to the people of this country. . . ." Yes (and here you could hear him take a deep breath), they were *all* back. (Later it was reported that the Czechoslovak delegation had refused to leave Moscow unless František Kriegel, one of Dubček's most faithful Presidium colleagues, would be permitted to join them. Kriegel, singled out as "that Galician Jew," had not been at Moscow's Vnukoro Airport when the others arrived to board their plane. The Soviets had kept him standing for six hours, hands up, facing a wall. He had finally joined his comrades at the airport, and only then had the delegation left Moscow.) The woman announcer, still crying, asked Smrkovský whether he had a message. He said, very quietly, they were exhausted, having gone two nights without sleep. Yes, President Svoboda would speak to the nation . . . and the others too . . . no, he couldn't say anything at the moment . . . this was no time to make a speech. Again he sighed, and said, "I believe we'll find a way," but he sounded hopeless and deeply depressed, and his listeners knew it. The woman thanked him. She sounded heartbroken. For her, and for millions of people who listened, this was the end of their hopes.

The Smrkovský interview was later rebroadcast. A commentator said that now all of them—Czechs, Slovaks, Poles, Hungarians, Ruthenians and everybody else—must stand together, more than ever before. "Keep a diary for the future, all of you, so that you and your children will always remember exactly what happened. And go back to work. That's the only thing we can do now." Ostrava said that the invalids of the Second World War had just started a new fund for the rebuilding of damages. A Polish speaker said, "The little people of Poland are with you, and they are waiting for their Dubček." Many towns asked urgently for asphalt to repair streets that were badly ruined by tanks and armored cars. In Brno, a Soviet tank outfit had disarmed the guards at the Czechoslovak Army barracks, and drove off with several Czechoslovak tanks. "The thieves even brought their drivers along because they knew our boys wouldn't drive." In Hodonín, the birthplace of T. G. Masaryk, there had been a clash between workers and Soviet troops. All workers were urged to remain "disciplined soldiers of freedom, to organize a warning service, and avoid quarrels with the Soviets. In Jihlava, the troops had occupied the Communist Party building "and acted like vandals in the printing plant of the Party paper." But another print shop was putting out a new edition. A firm in Moravia urgently asked for a shipment of chocolate powder or it would have to stop the production of chocolate ice cream.

It was reported that in Mestre, near Venice, a thief stole a car but left it near a police station with a letter of apology after he'd noticed the Czechoslovak (CS) license plate. The Youth Travel Buro announced that all scheduled trips to the Warsaw Pact countries were canceled. Photo amateurs were asked to get ready for a competition of "historical" photographs covering the invasion. At 11:20 a man told a reporter that the Russian soldiers had broken into his house in Pardubice, Bohemia, because he'd hung out a picture of Dubček. "They broke everything in our apartment. They didn't realize they did this to a worker." Radio Budějovice asked people not to stop trucks with wheat going toward the airport. "The wheat remains our property but must be stored temporarily in an empty hangar." Zemka Budějovice reminded Ústí of the promised delivery of oil.

A man introduced as "one of our leading actors" spoke on behalf of the country's actors and actresses.

> We are a little frightened by the size of the stage and the vastness of our audience but remember that we perform not only for this generation but also for the next. . . . Our houses remained dark for the past nights but each member of the large cast knows his part which is written by one's conscience. . . . Unfortunately the soldiers we see running around like badly coached supers are real life and blood soldiers. Friends, though we are actors, we know the difference between truth and make-believe. We know that we'll soon hear bad news. In this hour of our national tragedy all artists stand firmly behind our leaders. This awful play is written by history. Each of us has his role to perform in it. . . .

After a pause a man said, "Thank you, friend . . . Yes, we may have soon censorship of the press, of radio and television but we shall never have censorship of our thoughts."

A hotel in the Tatra Mountains offered "free rooms and good food to our tired leaders if and when they can afford a few days of well-earned rest." In Trutnow, Bohemia, Polish soldiers had told the people they were deeply ashamed and would never shoot at them. The "sacred truth" began to seep through layers of propaganda. In Plzeň, the workers had started a fund "for the support of free press and free information," and the local Communist Party contributed ten thousand crowns. (I remembered that several weeks ago *Literární Listy* had reprinted some angry letters from conservative groups, some of them workers, telling the editors, "you shouldn't have printed this." That, too, seemed to have changed in the past days.)

The station near Tábor was heard again with its fighting theme song, apologizing for being silent so long. A man in Prague said that Smrkovský had just crossed Prague on his way to the National Assembly (of which he is President), and had been given a tremendous ovation by the population. A bus driver got so excited that he departed from his route, with all passengers, following Smrkovský's car, but no one in the bus seemed to mind. For the first time in several days the bakers had made not only bread but also *jemné pečivo* (fine rolls). There were enough potatoes, no need to form long queues; the manager of a chain of markets expressed his thanks to the railroad workers who had worked day and night to distribute needed foodstuffs all over the country.

At 11 A.M. the Vienna Radio reported that "at least twenty-five people have been killed and three hundred and twelve wounded in Prague alone." Radio "Danube" reported that in Bratislava the Soviet soldiers had been completely demoralized by the nine o'clock demonstration, "going in tanks and armored vehicles through the streets like crazy racing drivers." Young people had told them that this was the "All aboard for Moscow!" sign. One tank drove into a car with four passengers. A man quoted from Lenin, "Communism is the highest expression of the human mind," and asked, "Did Lenin mean Dubček's or Brezhnev's or Ulbricht's Communism?" (The program was still a mixture of theory and practice. Technically, the relay was now working well, with stations blending in and out; there were now even conference talks between three or four stations.)

At noon, Radio Vienna interviewed a high-ranking tourist official from nearby Bratislava who had come on business and was going back there tonight. He said the Slovaks had learned a great deal in the past days.

> The little people, the common men know the truth now. No one talks about a separate Slovak state any more. We Slovaks are more emotional than our Czech brothers; often we listen more to our heart than to reason. We found it very difficult to restrain our hearts in these days. There were many who wanted to fight . . . but after the first two days they realized it would have been senseless to listen to the heart. We've learned through the hardest possible experience how much we belong together: through the blood that was shed by our patriots . . .

Radio Prague said that the National Assembly was still in session and "important documents might soon be read." All stations were asked to stand by. A man said that it was Munich all over again, "worse perhaps because in Munich no representatives of our people had been present, but in Moscow the painful compromise had to be signed by our leaders." He said he was going to read a letter which Karel Čapek had written after the Munich Pact,

> . . . and aren't we used to such blows of fate? Think of the Hussites when the whole of Europe was united against us, but we survived. During the Thirty Years' War, foreigners fought on our territory. We lost much of our population but against we survived. The human soul is the strongest weapon. . . . To believe in an ideal and live for it is everything. We have nothing to fear as long as we remain faithful to the heritage of hour tradition. . . . And we shall survive if we remain what we are . . .

At 12:40 Radio Prague began playing music. After a while, a man read from that morning's *Rudé Pravo*, "From now on we may not be able to say all we want to say, but we shall say

100

nothing against our conscience." Smrkovský was said to have reported to the National Assembly about the negotiations in Moscow. Radio Prague asked people not to call in now, since the two telephone lines had to be kept open for official use only. At 13:05 Prague broadcast Beethoven's Fifth Symphony. ("The hammering strokes of the orchestra seize us with weird, irresistible force," Paul Henry Lang wrote about the opening theme in *Music in Western Civilization*. This time the banal phrase of "fate knocking at the gate" sounded true. Was it an accident that they were playing Beethoven's Fifth, perhaps because they had no other recordings in their ersatz studio? Why didn't they play some Czech music? Was the ominous ta-ta-ta-*tah* to prepare the listeners for what was to come?)

A voice said, "Milada greets Božena," and then the opening theme was heard again. Then came the second movement, and the third; and still no word. Where were the brave men and women now who had literally kept the country going seven days and nights, since the first hours of the invasion? I've heard many performances of Beethoven's Fifth Symphony, but never one that seemed so tragic and so endless. After the third movement there were brief messages: "Pardubice needs coal urgently"; "The Plzeň Industrial School meets tomorrow at half past six in the morning for the hops harvest"; and a voice said, "Attention, Rudolf Cvik, collaborator, is on his way from Poprad (Slovakia) to the Soviet border—stop him before he gets there"; and then the fourth movement of the symphony was played. More news: a radio station in Bratislava was occupied, and the numbers of the tanks were given. The Hungarian station broadcast an appeal. I understood "Dubček" and "szabadság," which means "freedom." (The U. S. Embassy in Budapest is located in Szabadság Tér, Freedom Square.) Students of the Engineers' College were told to report to the dean's office. "Arnošt, call Ferda." I was beginning to miss the voices that had come through all the time. Where were they?

At 1:58 P.M. the harp melody from Prague was heard and a

man said: "An important announcement will soon be made, stand by." Ten minutes passed—and suddenly there was the exuberant beauty of Mozart's Jupiter Symphony. Why the Jupiter, one of the relatively few Mozart masterpieces expressing pure joy? Would there be good news after all? Or was it just another whim of somebody choosing the record at random? Mozart—the most beautiful voice of humanity. I switched to Radio Vienna where a man read from a Prague paper, "The real difficulties are about to begin now. . . . We must expect strong censorship again." Back to Radio Prague which made a short announcement at 2:25. Svoboda and Dubček would speak today, Černik and Smrkovský tomorrow. Once again, as at the very beginning, a woman announcer asked for "calm and courage."

(The official speeches of the Czechoslovak leaders were broadcast over the clandestine free network, the only one that was in touch with the entire population. It was the ultimate recognition for the "free, legitimate" Czechoslovak radio and the final admission of defeat, by the Soviet occupiers, who were unable to even provide a radio station after one week of military operations. There were now over 600,000 troops in Czechoslovakia.)

President Svoboda spoke to the nation at three o'clock. It was an old soldier's speech—brave and dutiful, not particularly exciting, important for what was left unsaid (but well understood) rather for what he said. Afterward there was a minute of silence. A woman's deeply depressed voice said, "This was a transmission from the Prague Castle." A melancholy piece of music by Dvořák was played.

Several Moravian stations were on the air. Various district leaders of the Communist Party refused any compromise. Radio Gottwaldov, the first station that had been heard after the invasion, said the workers demanded to know the full truth. "We shall accept no shameful betrayal." A man nearly broke down sobbing as he said that this was wrong, this must not happen. "He who sows the wind harvests the storm."

Other stations voiced strong protests. Was the nation going to disavow its leaders? Prague interrupted. A man implored the people to remain disciplined. The full text of the Moscow Agreement was not yet known. (Later it was reported that the Czechoslovak leaders were not even given a copy of the document which they had to sign at the Kremlin. It was a great day for Cossack diplomacy.) Svoboda's speech was re-broadcast. Suddenly, in the middle of it, it was interrupted. It was 3:35 P.M. Silence. Were the "free, legitimate" stations sabotaging the President's speech?

(Since then, the important part played by President Svoboda has become known. He is now a national hero, the second most popular leader—after Dubček—in his country. Throughout the drama, Svoboda has shown great dignity, courage and presence of mind. He has refused to receive Ambassador Chervonenko on several occasions, since he knew that Chervonenko was the man pulling the strings behind the planned puppet government of Alois Indra. If such a government had been set up, the Czechoslovak leaders—Dubček, Černík, Kriegel, Smrkovský etc.—were to be shot, probably in the lonely mountain villa near Mukačevo where they had been detained. Many people in Prague now claim that Svoboda threatened twice to shoot himself. Once before flying to Moscow when he demanded that all the other leaders must also come there. And then again, in Moscow, when he threatened suicide unless František Kriegel would also be permitted to return back to Prague with the Czechoslovak delegation. Kriegel had been tortured by the Soviets who considered him a "Zionist conspirator." People who later saw Kriegel in a Prague hospital report that for days he was unable to speak or to write, completely under shock.)

There was nothing but music until 4:58 when Prague was again on the air. The voices sounded different—revolutionary. They asked for the immediate departure of all troops, and repeated the decisions of the Fourteenth Party Congress that had secretly met earlier in Prague. A member of the Writers'

Union said defiantly, "We've written the truth until now, and we'll write the truth no matter what happens." Again a calm voice spoke up in Prague; there was always a voice of reason even in moments of emotion. He was pushed away by another man who called the youth of the country, pronounced the Party's disapproval of the Moscow documents and asked "for a return of the political situation prior to the occupation." For the moment, at least, emotion had overcome reason. The revolt seemed to be spreading to all parts of the country. In Plzeň, the writers *and* the workers at Škoda demanded that the occupying troops leave at once. Workers, writers, peasants, Party officials, scientists, individuals refused to accept capitulation. (I suddenly realized that no one had mentioned Dubček or Svoboda for an hour or more.) Confusion spread, and now there threatened chaos.

"Never give up!"

"Keep calm, friends, for goodness' sakes, keep calm!"

"No censorship—no capitulation!"

At 5:30 the Fifth Symphony was played again. This time the meaning was clear. A man speaking for the free radio said, "We shall not give up all we fought for in the past seven days and nights." At 5:50 P.M. the music broke off. A woman announced that Comrade Dubček would speak to the people.

Dubček's voice, too, sounded different. His delivery had often been businesslike, almost dull, though sometimes there were moments of subtle irony and wry humor. And always honesty and warmth, and people sensed it: this was no general, no politician, this was a friend. Now he started slowly, haltingly, often making sudden pauses, as though he had difficulty reading the script. Once or twice he stumbled and had to repeat a word. One could hear him breathing heavily. (At that time, none of his listeners knew that Dubček had gone through mental and physical torture in the past days and nights; he'd been kept incommunicado in various places, and he knew nothing of what was happening back home. He was not permitted to join the negotiations, until Svoboda made it an either-or issue, and many people think that Svoboda may have saved Dubček's life.)

It was a very bad speech but as he continued, he seemed to find himself again. There was the distinct echo of emotional shock in his voice as he spoke of the new "reality"—"reality" became the key word during the days that followed—and warned his fellow citizens against "anarchy." At one point his voice faded, and for twenty seconds, maybe more, there was a dead stillness. Later, it was reported that Dubček had been unable to go on with exhaustion and emotion, tears streaming down his face. When he said, "We are with our whole hearts behind you," one felt that he meant it, every syllable of it. I thought, if somebody can save this country from the worst now, it's Dubček. His words, like Beethoven's music, went "from the heart to the heart."

Pavel, the young medical student from Prague, called me in the evening. An older friend, L., under whom Pavel had served "in the upper Wenceslas Square area during the early days of the war" (válka), had just arrived in Vienna. Pavel spoke about Wenceslas Square as though it had been a battle-field, and perhaps he wasn't so wrong. I asked him to bring his friend over but he said, "I am already working, I got a job at the Vienna Fair carrying bags and pushing furniture. It's fine though, and many of the Viennese workers understand Czech, and we get along well." I asked him to come for fresh orange juice anytime, and he laughed and said he would.

L. came a little later, a slim, dark, intent man. He said he was born in Prague in 1933, the year Hitler came to power. When he was six, Czechoslovakia was occupied by the Nazis. He remembers the field-gray columns marching across the old, beautiful Charles Bridge. They looked impressive and he wondered why so many people were crying. Two years later he was taken with his parents to a concentration camp. After the war, he spent ten years working in factories. As the son of former bourgeois he was not permitted to go to the University. Later he made his studies, and by 1960 he had a good job, and was as deeply interested in politics as nearly everybody else in Prague. He joined Dr. Ivan Sviták, the political philosopher who formed the Club of Engaged Non-Party People (which many people in Prague, with the fine sense of semantic distinction in which the readers of Hašek and Čapek delight, call the "Club of Unengaged Party People"). Sviták amused Prague's intellectuals for years with provocative statements. A few weeks ago he declared, for instance, "I am a Marxist but not a Leninist."

No wonder the Sviták people were high on the list of the most wanted criminals by the KGB. On Wednesday morning, August 21, when a friend woke him up with the bad news at half past three, L. ran to the offices of the Club and began destroying membership lists and other documents. (Sviták happened to be abroad.) One copy of the membership list unfortunately remained at one of the very first buildings occupied by the Soviets but they haven't found it yet. L. heard that there was shooting near the Central Committee Building near the Moldau, and he went there. He saw the body of a woman who had been run over by a tank, and then more tanks closed in, and he ran away. By 8 A.M., when the Russians took over Radio Prague, L. had set up headquarters in a building overlooking the monument of Saint Wenceslas. Volunteers poured in all the time, young boys in blue jeans, hippies, minigirls.

"Everybody was welcome who offered help. We didn't even ask for their names. Of course, there might be a traitor among hundreds of people—but there wasn't." They set up two photo laboratories which were used by local photographers. The pictures were distributed among foreign [Western] journalists. By the second day, they had twenty photographers, a dozen people making press releases on several mimeograph machines, sixty boys and girls acting as messengers, who went to the underground newspapers and the free radio, and there was a large team making posters, banners, slogans. It was a large, well-organized group, and the Soviets who stood in the very front of the building and often were loitering inside the entrance, never found out about them. A special group of thirty girls was sent all over town begging for small contributions. They would buy bread, sausage, cheese, milk, so that everybody got something to eat twice a day. L. got in touch with four small printshops that would be ready to put out underground editions of newspapers and magazines at a moment's notice. "If a man came there with a certain codeword, they would take his material and get busy," says L. They even had cartoonists and artists. They put out the first "legal" (meaning, pro-Dubček, pro-resistance) issue of *Dikobraz* ("Porcupine"), a famous satirical weekly, on August 27. Its cover shows a small child threatened by five brutes carrying knives. Their similarity with Brezhnev, Gomulka, Ulbricht, Kadar, and Zhivkov is not coincidental. The caption says, "Tale of Five Brothers."

L. assigned a group of specialists to duty at the Saint Wenceslas monument. Every night the Soviets tore off the banners and slogans. Every morning L.'s young people put new ones up again. He often gave orders by megaphone, "like a director in silent films. Our aim was to make the houses disappear behind curtains of posters, slogans, banners. People would copy our ideas and imitate them in the outlying districts. There was no copyright; the more the merrier. Another group had the dangerous job of distributing the secret, legal newspapers all over Prague and getting them to the railroad men who would take them to the provinces, and in turn gave us provincial papers, for distribution in Prague. One fourteen-year-old boy was killed by the Soviets on the first day, in front of the monument. Later, a seventeen-year-old girl was wounded. Other groups were told to put up barricades, and to create confusion. We had some real experts. Boys would engage the tank crews in political, useless discussions, and meanwhile some mechanics would loosen the screws of the tank threads and do all sorts of things to immobilize the tanks. We had to be very careful though. The Soviets were brutal. I saw a boy killed who had carried our flag. They pierced him with their bayonets. Another man was shot ten meters from where I stood. We saw Soviet snipers on the roof of the National Museum. They shot at their own tanks to give the tank crews a reason for firing away. All of us are convinced that with very few exceptions no one in Prague shot except the Soviets who wanted to create incidents.

"A friend of mine saw a Soviet officer shoot one of his soldiers in Dejvice. Other boys witnessed the suicides of two Soviet soldiers. We started discussions with Soviet officers. They seemed to have small computers built into their heads. They spoke like the robots in Čapek's *R.U.R.* and had certain standard answers. After three or four days many Soviet soldiers were getitng afraid by the absurd situation which they couldn't control—the passive crowds, the hateful stares, people spitting upon their tanks. They had orders to shoot only when they were being attacked, but they didn't know what to do with people who got up on their tanks and set them afire. In front of the Law Faculty a soldier started to cry, and his sergeant quickly pulled him inside the tank."

L. decided to leave Prague when he noticed that he was being followed. It would take him at least one hour to get rid of some strangers. He doesn't think they were members of the Czechoslovak secret police. They wore cheap American-style suits and hats, "like Russians playing CIA men in a silly film." Most of the young people were unhappy that there was no armed resistance.

"The Soviets had it too easy. Their planes were coming in, minute after minute, flying low, as though they were kidding us. We got very angry. Some soldiers didn't bother to wear their steel helmets. Our nation lives on the memory of the Hussite wars, and now it will have to live on the memory of the glorious week of August 21. I've never known that people could get so close to each other, that they could be so good

108

and decent. Never before in all my thirty-five years did I have such a deep feeling of freedom, and such a love of humanity. No one was afraid. No one was mean. Oh, I know, you may keep it up for one or two weeks, but not for one or two years, and that's where the danger will come in. . . . But while it lasted, it was incredibly beautiful. We were happy as never before. I know that for all of us who were there it will remain the climax of our lives. . . ." He stared into space, and said, "I have no parents, no relatives, I have no money, no great future. I came out because I hope I can still *help* somebody, in some way. Back home, there is no one I can help now, and soon they would have to help *me*. I'll manage. You know, it's funny. If I had the choice tomorrow between a rich, comfortable life, or living through another such glorious week, I would do it all over again."

By Wednesday morning, August 28, most of the "free, legitimate" stations seemed to have disappeared into the air from where they had come. Radio Prague was still operating, giving some spotty news reports. There had been a meeting of the Czech journalists. ("We've listened to Dubček's speech and we are behind him. We know that there are many things he couldn't say.") A reporter of Radio Vienna had interviewed some students at Charles University. One said, "We are more afraid of the two hundred KGB men than of five hundred tanks in Prague." A worker at Škoda in Pilsen was quoted, "Round One is over, and the second round will be worse." Dubček's memorable speech seemed to have averted an open revolt. One station, which no longer identified itself, said, "We don't know how long we'll be able to broadcast. Some of our stations have already 'advisers.' We may have to be more cautious than we like to be." The Austrian radio said that the Czechoslovak borders were closed for all foreigners. No Western journalist was permitted to go there.

At 12:15 Radio Bratislava said the difficulties had become "insurmountable." They had to deal with coded messages and their telephones were tapped by the Russians. It was time to say goodbye. A woman said:

> We want to assure you that we will never betray you. We've become a living part of the nation and of the Communist Party. You gave us a mandate and we fulfilled it, day and night. . . . We promise you that we shall sacrifice for our nation, our legal organs, our Party, our citizens all our strength. If necessary, we shall give our lives.

A few other stations were still broadcasting but they gave only business messages or official statements. One station was playing the moving chorus of the Jewish prisoners from Verdi's *Nabucco*, the great song, "*Va, pensiero*," that had inflamed the Italians against the Austrian yoke in the late 1840s. At 5:40 a station calling itself "the Czechoslovak radio" (no longer "free, legitimate") broadcast a speech of Prime Minister Oldřich Černik. He sounded tired and uninspiring. A little later, the commentator in Prague whose relaxed, ironical comments in critical moments had done so much to help the people's morale, was on the air, for the last time. He sounded shaken.

> People, from now on you will have to think about what you read and hear. You've always been good at reading between the lines and listening between the nuances. Now our writers will have to practice the art of writing the truth by concealing some of it. Teachers, I hope you'll remember these days. Teach your pupils the truth and nothing but the truth for only those who know the whole truth will recognize even part of it. Educate the children in the spirit of freedom and humanity. You have a great responsibility to the nation. . . . Above all, let us all stay together now. At this time, no one should remain alone. Together it will be easier to endure. Workers, don't sell yourself—not for money, not for bonuses, not for better jobs. "Reality" does not mean capitulation; it

110

can mean honor too. To act rashly now would cause a
national catastrophe. People, love the truth. Remember the words we spoke to you on the first day of the
occupation: *klid a odvaha*, calm and courage. The
words remain the same. Calm and courage!

Realists to the bitter end, the people of Czechoslovakia
didn't blame anybody but themselves for their tragedy, the
third in their national history. There had been November 8,
1620, the Battle at the White Mountain. March 15, 1939, the
occupation by the Nazis. And now August 21, 1968. Not one
among the Czechs and Slovaks I talked to in Vienna commented
on the embarrassed silence of the United Nations, or on the
initial nonreaction of the United States. (Vienna's *Die Presse*
compared President Johnson's first condemnation, cautious
and mild, on the invasion, to Chamberlain's "Peace in our
time.") My friend J., the amateur historian, wrote, "I refuse
to accept the obvious, but illogical comparison between Vietnam and Czechoslovakia. Vietnam is a national tragedy for
the United States, and Czechoslovakia will be a tragedy for
the Soviet Union and world Communism. But there is a difference. After all, the United States did not invade France with
the help of the West German *Bundeswehr* and its other NATO
partners. France wants to quit NATO but *we* never wanted
to get out of the Warsaw Pact."

After two hundred and twenty-nine days, the "Prague
Spring" had come to an end. "We knew we would have to pay
a price for it but we didn't know the price would be so terrible," Smrkovský told the nation. People were already with-
drawing into silence and fear, and into the relative safety of
their private lives. From now on, no one would feel safe, while
the anonymous men in their "American-style" suits were
around. Moscow's *Pravda* demanded that forty thousand
"counterrevolutionaries" be "liquidated." (The language of
Himmler and Eichmann again.) *L'Humanité* and *Unità*, the
organs of the French and Italian Communist Parties, were no

longer on sale in Moscow. Vienna's Communist *Volksstimme* compared the anti-Semitic language of *Izvestia* to the *Stürmer*. In Moscow's Red Square, a small group of brave people unfurled banners "Hands Off the CSSR!" and "Long Live Free Czechoslovakia!" They were arrested and beaten, among them Mrs. Yuli Daniel, wife of the imprisoned Russian writer. Later they were exiled to Siberia, as during the Czarist rule.

In West Berlin, always a sensitive seismograph of Soviet power politics, worried people wondered what Ulbricht would do to them next. The Extra-Parliamentary Opposition, and many members of the New Left, after taking a long, deep breath, called the invasion "a brutal act of Soviet imperialism and the betrayal of Socialism." Germany's neo-Nazi NDP Party predictably supported the Soviet occupation. Erich Kuby, a West German writer who had been in Prague during the glorious week, asked in *Süddeutsche Zeitung,* "What would happen in West Germany in such a case? Some workers and leftist students would behave as the people of Prague and Bratislava. Others would hide or collaborate with whoever came along."

Not everywhere a clear choice was made by the New Left. Many vociferous Vietnam doves have remained strangely silent about Czechoslovakia. In neighboring Austria, people were informed by *Pravda* that American Green Berets were being trained in Salzburg for "action" in Czechoslovakia; a typical *Pravda* joke, perhaps, but no one in Vienna was amused. The papers reported that Soviet reconnaissance planes had "erroneously" flown deep into Eastern Austria. Later, the Austrians protested and the Soviets apologized, *after* their planes had taken a close look at Austria's airports and communications leading toward the frontier of Yugoslavia.

By the time the short Moscow communiqué was published, many people in the East and West had already written off Czechoslovakia. The Stalinist curtain had come down again. The economic outlook was desperate; the damages of the occupation were said to be close to a billion dollars and it would take years of hard work to get the economy into shape. Political observers predicted that the Soviets were skillfully engineering the destruction of Dubček and his boys. Sooner or later a Czechoslovak Kadar might appear on the political scene, or at least a Gomulka; how could Dubček maneuver between loyalty to his country, and Soviet pressure? Yet the only ones who are not pessimistic are the ones who lost most—the reformers, the writers, artists, scientists, and the young people.

"The renascence of Socialism has already a sound tradition in Czechoslovakia," Pavel Kohout, the author of the memorable Appeal, told Zurich's *Weltwoche*. "Occupation, brutal power and dictatorship are a terrible setback—but they cannot turn back the clock."

There are many Czechoslovaks who admit they were naive, expecting a miracle, hoping against hope. But there is nobody in this lovely and lonely country who will forget the "Prague Spring" and the glorious week that ended it. Brezhnev and *his* boys will be gone, but Jan Hus and Saint Wenceslas will still be there.

On the morning of Thursday, August 29, the "free, legitimate" stations seemed to have faded out. Radio Prague was there, calling itself again "Ceskoslovenský rozhlas," (the Czechoslovak Radio) as in "normal" times prior to the invasion. I called the monitoring section of Radio Austria and was told by an engineer that only one "free, legitimate" station was still broadcasting, probably somewhere near the Austrian border. "I'm afraid they're running out of power or something," the engineer said. "They're on 950 kilocycles. We can hardly hear them and we've got pretty good equipment."

I tried 950 kilocycles. The voices had died down to a whisper. After a while I got discouraged, and gave up. Temporairily, the sound of freedom had been muted in the lands of Jan Hus, Tomáš Masaryk, Alexander Dubček. *Bude tma.* It will be dark. But not forever.

K4

DATE DUE

7/2/70			
MAR 2 7 1971			
MAY 5 1971			
OCT 1 4 1971			
DEC 2 1971			
MR 5 - '77			
FE 4 '85			
GAYLORD			PRINTED IN U.S.A.